MAKE MATURE MULTIPLY

Becoming Fully-Formed Disciples of Jesus

EDITED BY BRANDON D. SMITH

Foreword by David Mathis

GCD Books is the publishing arm of Gospel-Centered Discipleship. GCD exists to publish resources that help make, mature, and multiply disciples of Jesus.

Cover design by Jeremiah Chaney
Interior design by Mathew B. Sims

To my wife, Christa, and my baby girl, Harper Grace. You two are my constant joy and encouragement.

And to the board, staff, and contributors of Gospel-Centered Discipleship. Your talent and hard work make my job easy.

TABLE OF CONTENTS

EDITOR'S PREFACE
Brandon D. Smith

As a new Christian, I was told that being a disciple of Jesus could be summed up in his own words—"If anyone would come after me, let him deny himself and take up his cross and follow me" (Mk. 8:34). While this statement is certainly a foundational truth of being a disciple, is this *it*?

In one sense, yes. Jesus could have stopped there and we could aim to model our lives after the self-sacrifice and humility he displayed on the cross. There would be nothing wrong with that. But he didn't stop there. Scripture gives us more. Much more.

The good news of the gospel is not only for self-application; it is for proclamation. It's meant to be shared. A disciple follows Jesus, invites others to follow him, and then trains them how to repeat the process. Simply put, disciples are called to *make, mature*, and *multiply* disciples.

First, we are called to *make* disciples. This means that we evangelize, we share the good news. Making disciples is about telling strangers, friends, family, and anyone else who doesn't know it yet that Jesus Christ is their King, their Savior, their God.

Next, we are called to *mature* disciples. So we don't tell people about Jesus and move along. We don't say, "I'm glad you believe! Enjoy yourself." Maturing disciples is teaching them to obey all that Jesus has commanded (Matt. 28:20). It's the process of sanctification—being made holy, becoming more and more like Jesus. We rely on God. We devour and dwell on the things of God found in the Scriptures. We pray. We kill sin in our lives. We serve others. We take "WWJD?" seriously by remembering *what he actually did*. These are but a few characteristics of a mature disciple. We model these things and we teach others to model them.

Finally, we *multiply* disciples. Mature disciples don't keep the good news of the gospel to themselves. Mature disciples, by the Holy Spirit's power, take Jesus to others. We are evangelized to evangelize. We are loved to love. We are forgiven to forgive. We are served to serve. We are redeemed to point to the Redeemer. We complete the cycle of discipleship by making disciples who make disciples who make disciples who make...

This is not a perfect process, but it doesn't have to be. Jesus was and is perfect so that you don't have to be. You can't save anyone, but you can show others the One who can. The Holy Spirit is with you (Jn. 14:25-26; 1 Cor. 10:13). My prayer is that this book will help you become a fully-formed disciple of Jesus who makes, matures, and multiplies fully-formed disciples of Jesus.

These chapters have been adapted from articles that originally appeared at GCDiscipleship.com. We like to think of this book as a "best of GCD" compilation. I speak for every contributor in this book when I say: we hope you see the glory of Christ on every page, and that you are so captivated by the beauty of the gospel that you can't help but take it to the ends of the earth.

Brandon D. Smith
Executive Director, Gospel-Centered Discipleship

FOREWORD
David Mathis

Once upon a time, evangelism happened on the church's own soil. She stood at the center of society. Most unbelieving Westerners had grown up in or around her, and felt some measure of comfort or nostalgia coming to a church building.

Occasionally, we might confront a non-believer on the street corner, or pack them into a stadium to hear Billy Graham, but in general, the work of evangelism happened in the church's own space. We invited them into our walls; some would agree to come. We put forward our best speaker to give his best gospel presentation. We'd even bring in a "revival" preacher from out of town. It was a restricted playing field, but it bore fruit in its time.

However, in the twenty-first century, the rules of the game are changing drastically, and fast. Increasingly, if we are to find the lost and win them to everlasting joy in Jesus, we must go find them where they are and engage them with "not only the gospel of God but also our own selves" (1 Thess. 2:8). No longer is it enough to man the church, put out an inviting sign, and wait for the lost to come streaming in. We must go meet them on their turf, out there in the world, and minister there—making, maturing, and multiplying disciples.

SENT INTO THE WORLD

Fortunately, all this hasn't caught Jesus off guard. He was ready all along for disciple-making in a society without the church at the center. This is what he had his disciples ready for in the first century, and prayed to his Father for them,

> I do not ask that you take them out of the world, but that you keep them from the evil one. They are not of the world, just as I am not of the world. Sanctify them in the truth; your word is truth. As you sent

me into the world, so I have sent them into the world. (Jn. 17:15-18)

Jesus's vision for his men has a different flavor than our well-worn line "in the world, but not of the world." His aspirations are higher. His accent is on another syllable. Instead of assuming we are "in the world," and now must labor to be "not of the world," he begins with the assumption that his disciples are "not of the world." And from there, he prays for them as he sends them into the world. The force goes in a different direction—not away from the world, but toward it. Not to avoid the world, but to win it.

And today, in the twenty-first century, we are beginning to experience more and more what it was like to be "sent into the world" in that pagan first century.

HELP FROM PHILIPPIANS 4:8

And so it is with Paul's wonderful coffee-mug encouragement near the end of his letter to the Philippians:

> Finally, brothers, whatever is true, whatever is honorable, whatever is just, whatever is pure, whatever is lovely, whatever is commendable, if there is any excellence, if there is anything worthy of praise, think about these things. (Phil. 4:8)

At first glance, this might seem like a circle-the-wagons manifesto. Batten down the hatches, keep your mind sealed off from the foul air of sinful society. Build the church walls thicker. Surely Paul is encouraging his readers to shelter themselves from society, right?

But growing number of careful exegetes are claiming that this verse is actually "designed to place them back into their world, even as they remain 'over against' that world in so many ways."[1] This text, rightly understood, may actually send us out

---

[1] Gordon Fee, *Paul's Letter to the Philippians*, NICNT (Grand Rapids, MI: Eerdmans, 1995), 414.

into society for the frontlines work of making, maturing, and multiplying disciples, rather than retreating to the bunker.

But don't take my word for it. Let's try to track closely with Paul's own intentions, rather than assuming that our English reading and Christendom mindset have gotten it right. There are at least three important things to point out in the verse.

"Consider" the Verb

First, even pastors with rusty Greek may recognize that the verb translated "think about" in verse 8 is not the one we would expect. The word here is *logizomai*, which typically conveys the notion of counting or computing. As one commentator observes, it is "unusual for Paul to use the verb *logizomai* with reference to a list of virtues."[2]

It would make more sense to us, perhaps, if Paul used the verb *phroneo*—"to set one's mind"—as he does in Romans 8:5 and Colossians 3:2. That would mean, as we typically have understood this verse, that we should give ourselves to pondering good, godly thoughts. But Paul doesn't actually say that here, though he could (as he does in other places). And we know Paul has the verb *phroneo* is at his disposal because he's just used it in Philippians 3:19 ("set their minds on earthly things) and elsewhere in the letter.

Instead, Paul goes with *logizomai*, which means to "count," "compute," or "consider." For instance, Romans 6:11: ". . . *consider* yourselves dead to sin and alive to God in Christ Jesus." Gordon Fee writes,

> What Paul says here is much less clear than the English translations would lead one to believe. The impression given is that he is calling on them one final time to 'give their minds' to nobler things. That may be true in one sense, but the language and grammar suggest something slightly different. The verb ordinarily means to 'reckon' in the sense of 'take into account,' rather than simply to 'think about.' This suggests that

---

[2] Moises Silva, *Philippians*, BECNT (Grand Rapids, MI: Baker, 2005), 197.

Paul is telling them not so much to 'think high thoughts' as to 'take into account' the good they have long known from their own past, as long as it is conformable to Christ.[3]

Paul's Odd Language
Second, Paul chooses some strange words as he rattles off six adjectives (in our English: true, honorable, just, pure, lovely, commendable) and two nouns (excellence, worthy of praise). At least these are strange for Paul. They are not the typical words he co-opts to characterize the Christian life in his other letters. Rather, they are words much more common to the unbelieving society in the first century than to the church. "The six adjectives and two nouns that make up the sentence are as uncommon in Paul as most of them are common stock to the world of Greco-Roman moralism."[4]

The "If Anything" Clauses
Finally, says Fee, this more missional reading "seems confirmed by the double proviso, 'if anything,' that interrupts the sentence." He continues,

> The six words themselves, at least the first four, already point to what is virtuous and praiseworthy; so why not add the proviso unless he intends them to *select out* what is morally excellent around them, and to do so on the basis of Christ himself? Thus, he appears to be dipping into the language of Hellenistic moralism, in his case tempered by Jewish wisdom, to encourage the Philippians that even though they are presently 'citizens of heaven,' living out the life of the future as they await its consummation, they do not altogether abandon the world in which they used to, and still do, live. As believers in Christ they will embrace

---

[3] Fee, *Philippians*, 415–416.

[4] Ibid., 415.

the best of what of that world as well, as long as it is understood in light of the cross.[5]

So, then, Paul is encouraging them in verse 8 "to take in account the best of their Greco-Roman heritage, as long as it has moral excellence and is praiseworthy."[6]

DISCIPLE-MAKING IN THE LIGHT OF THE CROSS

The implications of reading Philippians 4:8 this way then become a helpful guide for us, especially related to making, maturing, and multiplying disciples in our increasingly post-Christian context. First, Paul is calling us to embrace God's common grace at work in our surrounding society; regardless of what the doomsayers have told you, it's there to be identified and enjoyed—lots of it. But secondly, we must do so with discernment and Christian common sense—with the key being the very gospel that is the core and heart of all our evangelism and disciple-making.

It is hard to imagine a more relevant word in our postmodern, media-saturated world, where 'truth' is relative and morality is up for grabs.

The most common response to such a culture is not discrimination, but rejection. This text suggests a better way, that one approach the marketplace, the arts, the media, the university, looking for what is 'true' and 'uplifting' and 'admirable'; but that one do so with a discriminating eye and heart, for which the Crucified One serves as the template. Indeed, if one does not 'consider carefully,' and then discriminate on the basis of the gospel, what is rejected very often are the mere trappings, the more visible expressions, of the 'world,' while its anti-gospel values (relativism, materialism,

---

[5] Ibid., 416.

[6] Ibid., 415.

hedonism, nationalism, individualism, to name but a few) are absorbed into the believer through cultural osmosis. This text reminds us that the head counts for something, after all; but it must be a sanctified head, ready to 'practice' the gospel it knows through what has 'been learned and received.'[7]

And where the "anti-gospel values" are absorbed, the depth and duration of disciple-making is deeply compromised.

There's more to say in the pages ahead, but for now, let this summary lead us into our study: Paul's charge in Philippians 4:8 (and Colossians 3:2 and Romans 8:5, for that matter) should not lead us to isolate ourselves from our society and our Christ-given mission to go into it and make, mature, and multiply disciples. Rather, this text should have us leaning forward into it. This verse is a summons to make all of life, and all the world, our context for disciple-making.

As you consider evangelism and discipleship in the coming chapters, let me encourage you not to limit your vision to the walls of the church and the traditional categories. There is a place for formal meetings and classrooms and seminars. I love them. I teach them. I've benefitted unspeakably from them.

But as we disciple the nations, we will find that it requires not just the formal transfer of the gospel, but increasingly the informal sharing of "our own selves" (1 Thess. 2:8). The world is our classroom, as it was for Jesus and Paul. Let's consider whatever is true, honorable, just, pure, lovely, commendable, excellent, and praiseworthy in life and society; let's make disciples out there too, and model such engagement for those who will practice the things they have "learned and received and heard and seen" in us (Phil. 4:9).

David Mathis
Executive Editor, Desiring God

---

[7] Ibid., 421.

MAKE
DISCIPLES

1

WHAT TO DO WITH A TOLD GOSPEL
Jonathan Parnell

It was a beautiful Saturday morning, the kind nobody in Minnesota takes for granted. The sun was running strong, the air was happy, the sky had never been bluer. My family and I were finishing up breakfast outside when I opened the Bible for some kid-friendly devotional thoughts.

On this particular morning, our four-year-old was digging it. Maybe it was the change of scenery, or maybe the Fruit Loops, but something had her leaning forward, all ears. I was sharing about what it means to be messengers for Jesus in 2 Corinthians 5:20-21. The reason we had moved here, I explained, is because God wants our neighbors to know him. Plain and simple. We have good news, really good news—the kind of news that compels us to tell it. Then, the breakfast was over.

Within ten minutes, we closed down the cereal and laced up our shoes for a stroll around the block.

Elizabeth (our four-year-old) took one step out the front door and gladly bellowed, "Neighbors! Hey, neighbors! Come out! We're here to tell you about God!"

People heard her.

I've sat on this scene for months because, to be honest, I've not been sure what to do with it. What was she thinking? Was she street-preaching? Doesn't she get the value of relationships? Was she trying to give attractional ministry one last hoorah? I've mulled that picture over several times and tried to stamp it as cute but misguided. Admirable, but not serious. Deconstructing the zeal of a four-year-old—I know, it's embarrassing.

But here we are now. I think I get it. The fact of the matter, blaring the loudest that morning, is that a little girl bridged the most necessary application from *what I said* to *how she takes walks*. That is, she connected *what the Bible teaches* to *how she really lives* (and her dad has a lot to learn).

BELIEVING AND TELLING

Every Christian knows there is something about the gospel that drives us to tell it. There is some indivisible connection between believing it and making it known. It is good news, after all, and news is just that—*news*. Perhaps it would help, then, to re-highlight this simplest, most fundamental reason why we speak the gospel to others: because the gospel is essentially a told gospel.

There is good theological rationale here. One could start with what it means that God is a communicative agent. That he speaks and has always spoken in the intra-Trinitarian majesty of the Father and the Son by the Spirit. The knowledge of God's identity has always diffused itself. And undoubtedly, if this principle is found in his eternal essence, it will be detected in the preeminent word of who he is. More could be said here, but let's get to the Bible. Consider two texts.

> Great indeed, we confess, is the mystery of godliness:
> he was manifested in the flesh, vindicated by the
> Spirit, seen by angels, *proclaimed among the nations,*
> *believed on in the world*, taken up in glory. (1 Tim. 3:16)

This is a succinct dose of doctrine, perhaps a creedal formulation from the early church, maybe even a hymn. But whether that's the case or not, it's at least a memorable Pauline expression that distills the identity of Jesus into doxological prose. And essential to this confession of Jesus is that he is *proclaimed among the nations*. He is a spoken Jesus. A heralded King. One, in fact, who is heard and believed.

> And you, who once were alienated and hostile in mind,
> doing evil deeds, he has now reconciled in his body of

flesh by his death, in order to present you holy and blameless and above reproach before him, if indeed you continue in the faith, stable and steadfast, not shifting from the hope of *the gospel that you heard, which has been proclaimed in all creation under heaven,* and of which I, Paul, became a minister. (Col. 1:21-23)

Look closely at that phrase "the gospel that you heard, which has been proclaimed in all creation under heaven." Here's one of those rare exceptions where it helps to take a peek at the original language. John Piper explains:

The Greek for the phrase "which has been proclaimed" is *tou kēruchthentos*. This is a substantival participle which we could render "the proclaimed one" in English. It is in apposition with "the gospel" (*tou euangeliou . . . tou kēruchthentos*)—"the gospel . . . the proclaimed one."

Basically, Paul calls the gospel the "proclaimed-in-all-creation gospel." He refers to the gospel as what it is. The gospel is proclaimed. It is told. We don't get to opt out for a more myopic brand. There's no less expensive version without that feature. There's not a gospel for social butterflies and then another for introverts. Every one of us has only ever believed the told gospel, if we've believed the real gospel at all.

And the simplest, most natural implication of believing this gospel is that we ourselves tell it. We tell the good news in which we hope because hoping in told good news inevitably compels our telling it, too.

BUT THERE'S A PROBLEM

So then why don't we? According to a recent survey from Lifeway Research, we Christians don't seem to be telling people about Jesus very much. If we believe a "proclaimed-in-all-creation gospel," but we don't proclaim it ourselves, what gives?

Training, resources, equipping, examples—all of these are good and important. And we've seen a fair share of them the last twenty years. But what if it's simpler than that? (I'm speaking as a poor evangelist here.) Might it be that we don't tell the gospel because we're missing something in how we understand it? Maybe the lack of our telling it points to a deficiency in our grasp of its inherent tol*dness*? Maybe we've skimmed over the gospel's built-in compulsion to not just believe, but to believe and speak. Maybe the real need is not additional components of training, but deeper wonders to mine, depths by which to be overcome—so that the step from gospel to mission is not *a moving beyond* but *a moving further in.*

Do you know what God has done?

Remember the story of the sinful woman who washed Jesus's feet with her tears? She fell before him in awe, bewildered by his presence and mercy. And no one else got it. "This man isn't a prophet," the Pharisee criticized, "he doesn't know who this woman is!" The disciples may have been baffled, too, until Jesus tells a story.

Two men owed debts, one debt was a day's wage, the other a year's income. The debt of both men were cancelled, and Jesus asks which of these men would love the lender more. Simon responds, "The one, I suppose, for whom he cancelled the larger debt" (Lk. 7:43). Then we begin to see... the cluelessness of those bystanders corresponds to their ignorance of mercy. The crowd didn't understand the woman's devotion because they didn't understand what it means to be forgiven. That's why they responded so dumbly, so critical, so jaw-dropped and confused. Here was a reality—a beautiful, holy reality—that they could not wrap their heads around because they hadn't tasted the depths of Jesus's grace.

And maybe that's our problem with evangelism. We don't tell the told gospel because we've lost sight of what it means to be forgiven. All this talk of mission might as well be a broken prostitute washing Jesus's feet. It is nonsense to us unless we remember our debt. Unless we're flooded again with the news that it's cancelled—the news that it's cancelled, which we heard, which we were told.

The news that makes us step out the front doors of comfort and civility, and say, "Neighbor! Hey, neighbor! I'm here to tell you about God!"

2

HOW TO PROCLAIM JESUS AND MAKE DISCIPLES
Tony Merida

Him we proclaim, warning everyone and teaching everyone with all wisdom, that we may present everyone mature in Christ. For this I toil, struggling with all his energy that he powerfully works within me.
—Colossians 1:28-29

Recently our elders and a few of our interns made a trip to Boston in order to explore the possibility of helping plant churches in New England. While there, we visited some historical sites. One of them was in Quincy, MA, the birthplace of John Adams. Before going to see his home, we were told that in order to see where he was laid to rest, we needed to walk down to the Unitarian Universalist church (formerly a Puritan Congregationalist church). So we went inside and walked around. On the way out, some of our interns took a few pamphlets describing the beliefs of the UU. As we sat down for lunch, we began reading them to each other. The UU doesn't have a creed, so the statements are more personal opinions of its followers. Here are a few of them:

> [The] best of today's scholarship—which I identify with the work of the Jesus Seminar—reveals a man who is believable but problematic... he was best known as what we would today call a faith healer. His

"Golden Rule"—turn the other cheek, repay injustice with forgiveness—was youthful idealism not seasoned with wisdom. (Rev. Davidson, Loehr)

As a literal story the tale of Jesus's resurrection is hard to sustain, but as a metaphor that illustrates that there is life beyond death of addiction, despair, and total loss, it's hard to beat. (Rev. Lisa Schwartz)

All contributors [in the pamphlet] agree that the Bible is riddled with errors but nonetheless can serve as an important repository of human truth. (Tom Goldsmith, editor)

'If indeed revelation is not sealed,' then we must remain open to the possibility of new and higher truths that may come to us from diverse sources. . . including the Bible. (Mark Christian)

At sixty-nine, I now find myself almost never referring to the Bible for guidance or inspiration. (Jack Conyers)

I claim the Bible as one more chapter, among several religious texts, in the Unitarian Universalist guide to living. (Laura Spencer)

Yet the Bible remains for me but one rich source among many records that speak to us of the joys and challenges of being alive. (Rev. Donna Morrison-Reed)

What saddens me about these views isn't that people in the UU believe these things. I don't expect them to believe in the inspiration and inerrancy of the Bible, and a closed cannon. I don't expect them to believe in the deity and exclusivity of Christ, and his bodily resurrection. I don't expect them to read the Bible every day for guidance and inspiration. What saddens me is that many today seem to be functional Unitarians. I think the UU is a good representation for what a lot of people—inside and outside the church—actually believe. It's a religion based on one's feelings; one in which there's no absolute truth; a religion in which there are many ways to God; a religion in which you are free to live how you want, even if that lifestyle is contrary to the Bible. It's speculative, mystical, ambiguous, and ultimately Christless, making it useless. Why do I raise this problem? Because this is exactly why we need Christ-centered exposition today.

We are called to make disciples of all nations. As we go to the nations, we're sure to find "religious people," but we will rarely find a people who understand Scripture and the person and work of Christ sufficiently. Their beliefs will be similar to these mentioned above. We must take the truth of God's Word to them, just as Paul was taking the truth to the mixed up people in Colossae. Paul mentions four ways in which we do the work of Christ-centered exposition in order to make mature followers of Jesus in a diverse, confused, mixed up world.

PROCLAIM LIKE AN EVANGELIST

Paul uses the term "proclaim" (*kataggellomen*) meaning "to announce throughout," or "to proclaim far and wide." Paul is speaking of announcing the facts. Proclamation involves declaring the good news. This word is used in Acts 13 when Paul and Barnabas go out on their first mission. They went to Salamis and "proclaimed the word of God in the synagogues" (5). They heralded the facts in the synagogue. As faithful expositors, we get to say what God has said and announce what God has done in Christ. We are not giving advice. We are declaring the news.

We must proclaim the facts about Jesus because we believe that there is "salvation in no one else, for there is no other name under heaven given among men by which we must be saved" (Acts 4:12). Believe that the gospel contains converting power when you announce it (Rom. 1:16). I believe that exposition can be a life changing on the spot experience when the gospel of Christ is proclaimed. Don't merely preach about the gospel. Preach the gospel.

We also need to declare the facts about Jesus to correct popular ideas about him. There are numerous ideas about Jesus, displayed in world religions and pop culture. It's therefore imperative that the expositor understands the doctrine of Christ and salvation. The expository evangelist recognizes that there's no separation from theology and evangelism. Every evangelist does theology. The only question is whether or not they're doing good theology. Present the real Jesus to people.

Further, the evangelist must keep proclaiming Christ because this is the ultimate question for the skeptic. I remember talking to a guy in my office for about two hours one day. He asked me a bunch of questions, and then I finally said to my friend that the questions he must answer are questions related to Jesus (not whether or not Adam had a belly button or the historicity of dinosaurs). I told him these are the fundamental questions: "Who is Jesus?" "Did he rise from the dead?" Other questions aren't unimportant, but they aren't ultimate. Don't stop declaring the powerful truth of the cross and resurrection.

Tim Keller shares how a skeptic once told a pastor that he would be happy to believe in Christianity if the pastor could give him a "watertight argument." The pastor asked, "What if God hasn't given us a watertight argument, but rather a watertight person?" (Keller, *The Reason for God*, 232). Paul says that the Greeks look for wisdom, the Jews for miracles, but we preach Christ crucified (1 Cor. 1:22). I think the best way a skeptic to find Christianity compelling is by simply considering Jesus from his Word. Don't underestimate the power of plainly proclaiming Jesus weekly, and pray for the Spirit to open eyes for people to believe. Tell them to look to Jesus, to come to Jesus, to find their rest in Jesus.

Are you holding up the gospel for people to see and believe? I've always been challenged by Paul's words to the Galatians when he said, "It was before your eyes that Jesus Christ was publicly portrayed as crucified" (3:1b). He didn't mean that the Galatians were there at Golgotha, but rather that his preaching was so cross-centered that it was as if they were there! Take them there and urge them to repent and believe.

WARN LIKE A PROPHET

The next action word Paul uses is to "warn" or "admonish" or "counsel" (*noutheteo*). This word is often used of warning against wrong conduct (cf., Acts 20:31, 1 Cor. 4:14, 1 Thess. 5:12, 14, 2 Thess. 3:15). A primary role of the prophet-expositor is to warn people about false teaching and ungodly living. Paul uses this word for "warn" to the Ephesians elders saying, "Therefore be alert, remembering that for three years I did not cease night or day to admonish everyone with tears (Acts 20:31). I love that Paul says that he did the work of warning with "tears." Prophetic instruction should come from a deep, broke-hearted love for people. Jeremiah was the "weeping prophet." Jesus wept over Jerusalem. Be a broken-hearted prophet. Paul says, "I admonish you as my beloved children" (1 Cor. 4:14). Love your people deeply as you warn them about false gospels, the dangers of sin, God's judgment, and living in futility. As expositors, we can't be afraid to warn. Don't be naive or simplistic. Be aware of the dangers and threats and help people stay on the path of truth. A good expositor is like a forest ranger, aware of the landscape, alerting people to dangerous wildlife in the area. To put it simply, if you aren't warning people of heresy and ungodliness, then you aren't doing your job. Paul was often viewed a troublemaker because he wasn't afraid to sound the alarm. He warned of wolves and snakes in the area. Of course, to warn people is to confront people. This flies in the face of culture that loves its "autonomy" and "privacy." But that doesn't matter. We have to confront people with the truth of Scripture. A good shepherd will love his sheep enough to tell them the truth.

TEACH LIKE A THEOLOGIAN

The next way the expositor exalts Christ is through "teaching" (*didasko*). This refers to the skill of the teacher in imparting knowledge to the pupil. In proclamation we're announcing the facts, and in teaching we're explaining the facts. Paul's evangelistic outreach wasn't devoid of doctrinal instruction. He regularly taught, building up believers. Both are critical for the church's mission. We must reach the unreached people groups, proclaiming Christ where he has not been named, and we must teach and build up the church.

We need a generation of Christ-centered teachers. I love how Ezra "set his heart to study the Law of the Lord, and to do it, and to teach his statutes to Israel" (7:10). We need a generation like that! Paul tells Timothy, "Devote yourself to the public reading of Scripture, to exhortation, to teaching." (4:13). Be devoted to exhortation and teaching. Be immersed in it. Paul told Timothy, in his famous charge to "preach the word" to also "teach with complete patience" (2 Tim. 4:3). Notice how he adds "with complete patience." It takes time for people to understand gospel truths. The shepherd will feed the sheep bite by bite, over time, understanding the sanctification is a slow process.

I long for our people to have an "Emmaus Road experience" when they hear the gospel expounded from the text. The Emmaus disciples asked, "Did not our hearts burn within us on the road, while he opened the Scriptures?" (Lk. 24:32). May hearts burn as we explain the Holy Scriptures and point people to Jesus! After all, that's what we want from our teaching. The goal isn't merely to transfer information, but to have hearts filled with adoration. Exposition is for exaltation. Theology should lead to doxology. In good exposition, there are moments when people put their pen down, and stop taking notes, in order to behold Christ in worship. Theologian James Hamilton says, "The transformation the church needs is the kind that results from beholding the glory of God in the face of Jesus Christ" (Jim Hamilton, *God's Glory in Salvation*, 39). That kind of transformation will happen as we expound the Christ-centered Scriptures to people through careful theological teaching.

Make disciples of Jesus by proclaiming him like an evangelist, warning like a prophet, teaching like a theologian, and applying wisdom like a sage. Preach Christ until you die! Then worship him forever. Preach him on earth, until you see him in glory. I promise you on that day, you won't regret having done the hard work of Christ-centered exposition.

3

GOSPEL HOSPITALITY
Jeff Vanderstelt

Hospitality is a forgotten art. It also has a lost biblical history. We can recover the art of hospitality by understanding what it is and discerning how the gospel changes our notions of hospitality. In general, hospitality is about treating strangers as equals by creating space for them to be protected, provided for, and taken care of, followed by assisting and guiding them to their next destination. Let's see how this holds up to Scripture.

THE ORIGIN OF HOSPITALITY
There is a lot of history to consider in understanding the act or art of hospitality, but it all goes back to the beginning. In Genesis 1-2, we discern God's first hospitable act. Consider what God did when he created the world and the Garden of Eden for humanity to live in it. He gave Adam and Eve all they needed to enjoy life restfully while doing the work he created them for. He gave them space to exist, to enjoy creation, and to enjoy each other and fellowship with him. They were given both the space and the capability to create, to work, and to exercise authority, with all the resources necessary.

ISRAEL: GOD'S HOSPITABLE PEOPLE
Consider God's commands to his people regarding hospitality to strangers (Lev. 19:9-10, 33-34; Deut. 10:18-19). Through Abraham and Sarah, God created a new nation—a People blessed to be a blessing to all nations. He gave them all the resources and

capabilities to exercise hospitality to strangers, orphans, and widows. Similar to the Garden experience, Israel offered his people a place of refuge where others could rest and receive all that they needed, enabling them to do what God had created them to do. However, now this rest came in the midst of a broken, sinful world.

On the flip side, think of the number of occasions where Israel found itself as strangers among a host people. In some cases, they found a hospitable reception (Egypt with Joseph in charge; the spies and Rahab). In other cases, they found themselves treated like enemies or slaves (slavery in Egypt; Babylonian captivity). God had called them to be hospitable, yet they often failed to do so. After receiving hospitality, this must have become clearer to them.

God allows us to experience grace as recipients so that we might be distributors of grace to others. Hospitality toward Israel was a clear example of God's gracious gift, once again, and should have motivated generous hospitality. Unfortunately, Israel failed to enter God's rest because of their unbelief and disobedience (Heb. 4). So, they not only failed to rest in the work of God, but also failed to offer that rest to other nations. In all their hospitable failures, they needed one who would fully rest in God in order to become an enduring place of refuge for others.

RETHINKING HOSPITALITY WITH JESUS

Jesus entered into a culture shaped by a variety of world views (The Imperial Cult, Jewish Monotheism, and Hellenistic Philosophy, to name a few). In this culture, the concept of hospitality was rooted in several different traditions. First, the idea of taking in a hostile stranger or enemy and treating him as you would yourself. Second, the Greek practice of hospitality in which a stranger passing outside a Greek house would be invited inside the house by the family. The host washed the stranger's feet and offered him/her food and wine. Only after the stranger was feeling comfortable could the host ask his or her name. This practice stemmed from the thought that the gods mingled among men, and if you played a poor host to a deity, you would incur the wrath of a god.

A third shaping force in the concept of hospitality in Jesus's day was the Hebrew understanding (as briefly considered in the passages above and demonstrated also in the story of Lot and the angels in Genesis 19). Jesus comes into this cultural context and calls the weary to himself, feeds the hungry, mends the broken, eats with sinners and tax collectors, washes his disciples' feet, and ultimately gives his life to cleanse us from sin, deal with our unbelief, and provide a way and place for us to rest. Jesus lives, loves, obeys, works, dies, and rises again so that we might find a place of rest, renewal, and recreation. He offers us rest in order to send us on our way to be about God's purposes—rescued to offer rest. Jesus saved us to be his hospitable people!

3 WAYS THE CHURCH CAN BE HOSPITABLE

In light of the Gospel, we might define hospitality as the creation of a space that allows people *to be themselves, to become renewed,* and *to do the works* God has saved them for. When we properly exercise hospitality, we welcome people to be themselves in the warmth of the light of Christ, to become renewed by being changed by the work of Christ, and to do works we have been created for in Christ.

1. To Be Rested

In a broken world, marred and diseased by the effects of sin, people need the space to rest. This is why Jesus called people who were weary and heavy-laden to come to him. He would give them rest for their weary souls. Jesus calls us to rest in his work on our behalf. This way, we can be a people at rest who provide sanctuaries of rest for others.

Before the Fall, Adam and Eve were naked and unashamed. God had created a place and made space for them to be themselves without covering or facades. If we are in Christ, we are clothed with his righteousness. We don't need to cover up or hide. One of the ways we create space for people to experience and come to understand the gospel is by creating space for people to reveal their true self and see that they are loved regardless of the "wrinkles and scars" of sin. How do we create space for people to be their true self?

2. To Become Renewed

The gospel isn't *only* about loving and forgiving sinners. It is also about restoring broken and marred people into healed and whole people who grow up to become imitators of Jesus Christ—restored image-bearers of God. Jesus created space for people to be and to become (Think of Mary, Peter, Thomas, the woman at the well, the blind man, the paralyzed). Gospel hospitality implies creating space for people to be known, to be real, to be loved, and ultimately to be led with the Holy Spirit's help to healing and wholeness through the person and work of Jesus Christ. How do we create space for people to be led toward healing and wholeness?

3. To Do Works

The gospel moves from who God is and what Christ has done on our behalf into the works he created us to do (see Eph. 2:8-10).

This is the result of Jesus's gospel hospitality. He got on the same level with his enemy by becoming human. He became our servant to the point of death. He spent all that he had in order to clean us up by becoming our sin and giving us his righteousness (2 Cor. 5:21). Then he sent us his Spirit to empower us to do good works for his sake so others could be welcomed in to the family. When we engage in gospel hospitality, we are regularly asking ourselves this question:

How do we create space for the stranger to be rested, restored, healed, and prepared in Jesus Christ for the work God has called them to?

Will you join God's rich history of providing rest in order to extend rest? Remember, everything he has called you to do he has already done for you in Christ Jesus. You have everything you need to offer gospel hospitality to the strangers, friends, and even enemies around you.

4

EVANGELISM HAS BECOME A DIRTY WORD
Matt Brown

Evangelism has become a dirty word. This is probably because of situations like my wife and I ran into in San Francisco a couple years ago. We spent a few days traveling up and down the Pacific Coast Highway before working at the Oracle Conference, a technology conference attended by more than 30,000 business people from all over the world. As we walked to the convention center from our hotel one day, I noticed a short, stalky gentleman on the street corner in the midst of all the hustle and bustle.

Suddenly, the man on the street corner began to scream. It was not your average yip or yell. It was a high pitched, throaty kind of scream, one that would cause you to lose your voice within a few minutes of unleashing it. He began to wave his Bible back and forth in the air. Between his gasps for breath, I could tell he was saying something about Jesus, repentance, and God. The crowds quickly skirted around him, crossing the street as fast as they could, adding one more reason to their dislike of the "E-word."

As I've gone back over this experience in my mind, my main deduction is that this stalky street preacher was using the wrong bait.

Jesus talked to his first followers about "fishing for men." I'm not much of a fisherman myself, aside from the occasional sunny day in Minnesota (we have 10,000 lakes in here, so it's almost a sin not to do all that fun lake stuff). If fishing has anything to do with the "E-word," we can easily assume that "different strokes work for different folks." It doesn't take a brain surgeon to discover that screaming at a businessman (or 30,000 of them) is among the most unsuccessful sales pitches in the history.

I get it. I understand why evangelism has become a dirty word, but I want to believe God can do something different with it through my life. If I don't scream the gospel, what can I do? How can I care about people more authentically, love people more unconditionally, and share the gospel more faithfully?

SO WHAT DO WE DO?

We have to put ourselves in the apostles' shoes. When they traveled with Jesus, what did they say? What did they do?

I've done my fair share of street evangelism. It took me many years to realize something profound: the first followers of Jesus did not witness to every person they met on the street. In my mind, I had somehow come to the conclusion that the more we witness to strangers, the holier we become. I used to think that if I could just witness to literally every person I came into contact with throughout my day, I would have made it into Kingdom greatness. (I seriously thought this.)

It took some time and some years to understand Acts 17:2:

As his custom was, Paul went into the synagogue, and on three Sabbath days he reasoned with them from the Scriptures.

What did Paul do on the days in between? We don't exactly know, but we see on every church day, he took opportunities to speak of Christ, proclaim Christ, and call men and women to Christ. Paul wasn't rabidly evangelizing every single person he met throughout the week (although he clearly did personal evangelism at times), yet in the power of the Spirit, the spread of the gospel was the driving force of his life.

The gospel frees us from the notion that the evangelization of the world falls on our shoulders alone.

I believe in reaching the world. I believe that God has placed each of us in the time we live in, growing up where we grow up for a reason (see Acts 17:26-28). But it is God alone who draws men and women to himself (Jn. 6:44), and it is the Church collectively that is called to reach the world. Not me. The Church together. With every part working its unique strength (Eph. 4:16) that God can use for his glory.

We can play a small part in God's grand story: the rescue and redemption of the world. Our role is led by the Spirit and focused on Christ. We carry it out by setting apart Christ as Lord within our own hearts, to give an answer to anyone who asks for the hope we have received, and to always share of Christ with gentleness and respect for our hearers (1 Pt. 3:15). Our role is to be faithful to the leadings and promptings of the Holy Spirit in the large and small stages of our lives. If we are to "do the work of the evangelist," we must study the life of Christ, and also the story of Philip the Evangelist in Acts 8. He was led at key moments by the Spirit, where to go, what to do, what to say. He was prepared with a proper understanding of the Word of God and how to point a seeker towards Jesus.

WE DON'T GO ALONE

Evangelism becomes a dirty word when it is done religiously out of human motivation (often guilt and aiming to earn God's pleasure by works) and attempted to be accomplished through human strength. *The antidote comes from understanding our proper role as simple tools in the hands of God.*

> One says, "I follow Paul," and another, "I follow Apol-los," are you not mere human beings? What, after all, is Apollos? And what is Paul? Only servants, through whom you came to believe—as the Lord has assigned to each his task. I planted the seed, Apollos watered it, but God has been making it grow. So neither the one who plants nor the one who waters is anything, but only God, who makes things grow. The one who plants and the one who waters have one purpose, and they will each be rewarded according to their own labor. (1 Cor. 3:4-8)

The message of evangelism is not just "go," but also, "I am with you always" (Matt. 28:19-21). It is Christ's presence that heals. It is Christ's presence that saves. It is Christ's Presence that delivers. We are needy of his presence every day in every way. Unless God moves, and does through us what he loves to do best, hearts will remain darkened to the light of the gospel.

5

5 BOLDNESS-INCREASING QUESTIONS
Jeremy Writebol

I don't know anyone who sees evangelism as an easy task. For most of us, the work of declaring the gospel to our lost friends, family, neighbors, and co-workers makes us quake in our boots. If you and I are anything alike, we would have to confess that sharing the good news of Jesus makes us timid.

Maybe it's justifiable, in a sense, given the political and moral climate of our world today. It seems that the only thing our world can be absolutely positive about is that there are positively no absolutes. Anyone who expresses a dogmatic claim to "big-T" truth is an arrogant intellectual Neanderthal of a bygone era. Expressing that a differing position, especially on religious matters, could be wrong and even subject to eternal judgment is the social *faux pas* of our day. It's no wonder we can be timid about sharing our faith.

INCREASED BOLDNESS

I struggle with my own fearfulness about sharing the gospel along like anyone else. Yet recently, the Lord has not only placed opportunities but encouragement in front of me to be about declaring his love in the life, death, and resurrection of Jesus to those who don't believe. The encouragement has come through his Word, specifically Acts 4.

The passage is filled with the tension of a secular, religiously liberal leadership struggling with the exclusive claims of uneducated, common men declaring Jesus as Lord. A healed cripple stands before the midst of the forum on religious tolerance as evidence for the minority opinion. And like a blast of cold water to my face, I'm confronted with questions that give me an adrenaline shot of confidence.

Layered beneath an arrest, trial, confession, and regrouping phase are five questions for us to ask ourselves. If we answer them correctly the measure of our boldness to proclaim the gospel will only grow.

1. WILL GOD SAVE?

As Peter and John declared that the resurrection of Jesus was the power source behind healing the cripple, the assault mounted. If there was ever a time to back down and disperse quietly into the streets of Jerusalem, now was the time. And yet they stayed, preached Jesus, and ended up in a holding cell for the evening. By modern standards, their work was a failure. Now they have been identified and are in the beginning phases of a lifetime of persecution. But Acts 4:4 tells us that something amazing occurred in the midst of their suffering and teaching: people came to Christ. People were saved. As the gospel was under attack, it was also advancing and moving forward.

How does asking this question increase our confidence and boldness in witness? It reminds us of what and who we are not. We are not God. We can't save anyone. No matter how clear our presentation of the gospel, no matter how effective our technique or delivery of that message, we can't take the heart of a spiritually dead person and bring it back to life. Only God can do that. And God does that through the declaration of his good news of Jesus. God is the one who saves. Not us. And so boldness grows because we know the one who brings salvation.

But not only is he one who brings salvation, he is the one who promises to bring salvation. His word tells us that "faith comes by hearing and hearing through the word of Christ" (Rom. 10:17). People will come to faith in Jesus by our declaring the good news of Jesus, even in the face of opposition and suffering. We can be bold because God has promised to save sinners and he actually does so!

Is God able to save my lost neighbor through my imperfect, inadequate, inarticulate sharing of the good news of Jesus? Yes,

yes he is. So I can be supremely confident that God will do what he has promised. Will God save? Yes he will. Yes he does.

2. HAS GOD SPOKEN?

The second question is a further injection of boldness into my spiritually-timid heart. A major source of fear in sharing the gospel is the fear of speech. Folks will often say, "I just don't know what to say to them." There is a fear of saying the right things (or even the wrong things), and that the message of the gospel won't be clear and straight and helpful.

As Peter and John were dragged before the Sanhedrin to testify, they were at a clear disadvantage. These two poorly educated, common, blue-collar fishermen were standing before the educated, intellectual, political influencers of their day. If they were ever going to feel over their heads, this would be that time. And yet God's promises were evident and real within them. Peter, filled with the Holy Spirit, opened his mouth and boldly, clearly declared the gospel. Making one of the most exclusive statements about the authority and centrality of Christ in all of the Bible, Peter told the religious pluralist of his day that there is salvation found in no one else except for Jesus (Acts 4:12).

Where did he get this confidence? It came from the emboldening reality that Christ promised to speak through them. He told them not to worry when they stood before rulers and authorities and powers because the Holy Spirit would give them the words to speak (Matt. 10:19-20).

We too can have this same confidence to speak the good news of Jesus because we too have the gospel word. We have Christ, who is the living, breathing, flesh-and-bone Word of God, to declare to our unbelieving friends. We don't have to invent the message or come up with clever or memorable ways of stating it; we can simply declare the Word of Christ to them. This doesn't mean the gospel is reduced to a formula or a small track of information, but that as we live life among unbelievers, we don't have to rely on a style of delivery to bring them to faith and repentance. We rest in the power that God supplies as we declare the perfect life, substitutionary sacrifice, and powerful resurrection of Jesus for us and our salvation. God speaks through his Word. He speaks today and he will speak to those who don't know him.

3. HAS GOD SENT?

As Peter and John confidently proclaim Christ as Lord to the religious liberals of their day, the basis of their authority was called into question yet again. These powerful, political Jewish leaders could not understand how common, uneducated men could teach with such authority and conviction. They were frustrated that the apostles were without credentialed papers or authorization to preach such a message. If the lowest form of leadership influence is to stoop to a title earned or positional posture, then the Sanhedrin had only one card left.

After hearing the testimony of Peter and John, the Sanhedrin sent them away and deliberated how to stop this Spirit-led movement. They decided to tell the apostles to stop declaring their bold, exclusive message of Christ. Once again, the opportunity to capitulate to the religious leadership was there. Peter and John could have backed off and said, "They just want us to stop talking about Jesus. Okay, be we can still tell them God did it." And yet, Peter and John knew where their authority was derived. They were authorized and sent by Christ himself to witness about him. They knew they had a mission and that they had two options: either be faithful to the one who sent them, or disobey and disregard the authority of Jesus who sent them.

Boldness grows within our own lives when we see that we too have been sent by Christ for the exact same mission. Just as Jesus sent his first disciples to go and make more disciples, this mission still stands for us today. We are called to obedience and faithfulness in the work of that mission. As a prominent pastor used to say, "We are either missionaries or impostors." We have a mandate to take the word of Christ and witness to his resurrection to the world in which we live.

How can I be confident or bold in sharing the gospel with those around me? It stems from knowing the one who sent me and knowing his call on my life to witness to his grace, power, and love. Peter and John declared, "We cannot but speak of what we have seen and heard" (Acts 4:20). Why? Because they had been sent.

Where do you live today? Where are you at right now? Do you see that God has sent you to that place? Do you understand that Christ has, by his authority, placed you in that specific place and within those specific relationships with the mission of sharing about him? Boldness can grow when we see our calling and our mission in this light. We are sent to these people at this specific point in human history to declare to them the cross and resurrection of Jesus on their behalf.

4. WILL GOD SUPPLY?

With a healed man who had been a cripple for over forty years of his life standing before them and two men boldly proclaiming Christ, this council had no way of outright punishing Peter and John. All they could do is send them away with greater threats and a promise of greater persecution. Again, this was another opportunity to cower in fear, to back off the message, or to bow out altogether.

As they went home to their family and friends, the adrenaline rush of being in prison and before a council that could call for your death began to wear off. Maybe this was too risky of a move. Maybe the church should drop down undercover for a while. Maybe the cost is too high. As they gathered the church together, the threats could become deafening, forcing them to press pause on the movement. And yet the calling stood before them. So they asked a fourth question. Will God supply the very thing we need, namely boldness, to continue witnessing to the gospel of Jesus in the face of persecution?

Will God supply what we need? The early church assembled together and prayed and asked for that very thing in Acts 4:24-30: "God supply what we need. Give us more boldness." How do you increase in boldness? You ask for more of it. To be bold declaring the gospel, we need to ask for God to supply the boldness we lack.

Maybe we are so nervous about sharing the gospel because we haven't asked for the Spirit to empower us in the mission.

We haven't asked for God to make us bold. Even in the face of the threats, whether real or imagined, we have simply forgotten the one who has all authority and power and the one who will accomplish his mission (Matt. 28:18). Boldness comes if we ask for it.

I love verse 31 of Acts 4: "And when they had prayed, the place in which they were gathered together was shaken, and they were all filled with the Holy Spirit and continued to speak the word of God *with boldness*." They prayed and God gave them the very thing they asked for.

Will God supply what we need to be faithful in the mission he has given us? If it really is his mission, then how can he deny us what we need? We just have to ask.

5. DO I TRUST GOD?

This brings me back to asking one all-encompassing question to increase my boldness. Do I trust God? Will he do what he has promised (save) by the means he has ordained (speaking) to the people he has placed before me (sent) in the power he gives (supply)? If I can answer yes to that one question, then I am emboldened to do what he calls me to do.

This isn't a matter of conjuring up my own faith and motivation. It's the question of my heart saying, "Lord, I believe. Help my unbelief!" (Mk. 9:24). Do we trust God to do what he has promised to do? Then let us with courageous boldness ask him to continue saving, speaking, sending and supplying us with boldness for his glory.

6

HOW TO TELL THE BETTER STORY
Logan Gentry

Evangelism might be the most discussed, most intimidating, and least discussed practice in the American church. When church finished our sermon series through the Sermon on the Mount, I was amazed by how Jesus evangelized through his message and his life.

It can be easy to view the Sermon on the Mount as directed simply to believers, but Jesus's view was beyond the disciples sitting with him; it involved the non-believing, curious, and even the antagonistic crowd around him. He doesn't supply a complete explanation of any of the topics he addresses. He spends two verses dealing with divorce, makes simple statements about how we should use our money, and provides a small insight on anger and lust being rooted in the heart.

In all of the issues Jesus addresses, he is presenting a better story, a better narrative to follow than the world offers. It truly is picture-perfect evangelism, declaring through "you have heard it said, but I say" statements that contrast the cultural narrative lived around us and the kingdom life he brings. This must guide us as we process how we have been evangelizing, and how we can move forward evangelizing and proclaiming the gospel of the kingdom of God through Jesus Christ.

THE GOOD NEWS
We must ask whether we truly believe that the gospel is good news in our lives, and if it is the prevailing narrative that we live for. If it's not a better story, bringing greater peace, joy, and

hope in the midst of whatever circumstances come, then how can we invite people to believe it as better for them?

When we follow Jesus and the life he offers, evangelism flows from a natural expression of the change we are continually experiencing.

For example, when I go see a basketball game with one of my son's classmates' dad, and we begin to talk about our kids, I am confronted by whether the gospel has been guiding my parenting. If it has been guiding my parenting, I can acknowledge with him my failures in disciplining without patience and love at every moment, but also explain how the gospel guides me in interacting with my son. I get to explain that I can affirm my love for my son rooted in him being my son, not in his performance.

I can also describe how my desire in correction is that my son would know the delight and joy in obedience rather than the destructive nature of sin as he trusts Jesus and his parents. This presents a better story than our culture's typical annoyance by kids' rambunctiousness, disobedience, and anger in timeouts or discipline, and points to the responsibility of the parent to lovingly correct and teach a better way of life by correction and modeling. It also demonstrates and aims to highlight that this can only be done well through gospel motivation and empowerment by faith.

THE GOSPEL IS THE BETTER STORY

Jesus's words in the Sermon on the Mount sound impossible to follow at times, but thankfully he fulfilled all of the demands and challenges that he presented for us through his flawless life. His fulfillment is now imparted to us by faith in his death and resurrection through the Holy Spirit to empower us to live the better story so that it becomes a better and ever-increasing reality.

Jesus speaks to so many areas of our life, and provides a better way forward than the one typically based on life experiences, preferences, and at times, heritage. If we never stop and consider how Jesus calls us to live differently from the desires of our heart, to the private and public expression of our faith, we will not be able to share how the gospel transforms our approach to relationships, career, and even the religious devotion we are hoping our friends and family embrace. The call is to vibrant faith rather than dead religion. And only the gospel produces that in us.

THE BETTER STORY DEMONSTRATED

Jesus proclaimed the Sermon on the Mount, dropped the microphone, walked off, and lived it out. When we invite our neighbors to see the better story played out in the community of faith through parties, meals, and service to the neighborhood, our words have more power based upon the life that is formed through them.

This is where evangelism becomes easier and normal. You are already doing and being a part of environments in your faith community where evangelism can happen, but you've forgot to provide the invitation to those who don't know the better story yet. Jesus invited the crowds to follow him as he lived what he taught, and in doing so, informs us that we get to evangelize by presenting a better story through everyday life.

My hope is that the church embraces Jesus's words as the greatest story ever lived. I pray that we enjoy it, and through loving it, we live it out as a powerful proclamation to our friends, co-workers, and family.

EXAMPLES OF TELLING THE BETTER STORY

I thought I would provide a few real life questions and scenarios to help.

1. I met a pro-choice advocate asking if I supported women's rights for abortion. They asked, "Are you against abortion?" Obviously, this is a potentially heated debate with a lot of emotions. I chose to answer like this: "I believe there can be a better way. What if there was a community that would adopt, care for, and raise that child and the mother/father could be a part of their lives? This is God's desire for the people of God, to assist families and care for any and every vulnerable child."

2. After finding out I'm a pastor, I've been told multiple times, "So you believe I'm going to Hell." Always a great conversation starter. One way to present the better story would be to say, "I believe you don't have to go there. Christ took all the punishment that you or I deserve by dying on the cross. He provides a way for us to know him in relationship, to know true joy, and to experience Heaven now and to love him forever."

3. An even more common occurrence that I've seen in my life and our community is that social events are for everyone, not just Christians. Show the joy of Christian community by inviting them to the party and demonstrating the same relationships, conversations, and care for others that you do in fellowship with Christians.

Jesus and his Kingdom is the better story and better reality for our day. It's yours by faith and offered to anyone who will receive it.

7

INVITE AND INVEST TO MAKE DISCIPLES
Greg Gibson

As Jesus completes his public ministry and prepares for his crucifixion, resurrection, and ascension, he spends his final moments with his disciples—teaching them what it means to abide in him and be his disciples on mission in the world. John 14 -15 provides a clear understanding of what it means to abide in Jesus.

Based on this text, I use two questions to develop a common language for discipleship within my church community: "Are you abiding in Jesus Christ?" and, "Who are you teaching to abide in Jesus Christ?" When we teach others to abide in Christ, we follow a very simple pattern of inviting them into relationship, investing our time and lives in them, and imagining with them what their lives would look like if lived in light of the gospel.

INVITING
In John's Gospel, you see a very simple yet profound practice that Jesus employs in order that his mission will continue on after his death and resurrection: *the practice of invitation.* In John 1:35-51, Jesus extends the invitation to Andrew, Peter, and Phillip by simply calling them to "Come and See" and "Follow Me." Although these would-be disciples have no idea what is in store for them, they drop what they are doing and begin the journey of learning from Jesus.

If your aim is to make disciples, this practice is essential for you as well. I believe the simple and intentional practice of extending an invitation to another person in order to teach them the truth of Christ and model for them a life in Christ is what is often missing in our attempts to make disciples.

We may talk about making disciples and even hope to make disciples, but until we actually invite someone to become a disciple, we have only a stated value, not a true value.

If you were to invite someone to be a disciple and teach them what it means to abide in Christ, who would it be? Perhaps a struggling couple in your church, a neighbor down the street, an unbelieving co-worker, or even the barista at your local coffee shop? Begin to pray and ask the Holy Spirit to lead you to someone you can disciple—and when he does, extend an invitation.

INVESTING

Jesus spends an inordinate amount of time in John 13-17 alone with his disciples. Since he has completed his public ministry, and since he knows that he will soon be put to death publicly, he takes a large amount of his time investing in his disciples.

The practical impact of this text cannot be overlooked. Think about all of the "good" things the Incarnate Son of God could have been doing with his last few moments of "free time." he could have continued healing the sick; he could have continued calling the masses to faith and repentance; he could have even continued pleading with the Pharisees to turn from their religion and embrace him as the Messiah. But he doesn't do any of these things.

Instead, Jesus invests the fading moments of his earthly existence with 11 (Judas has since departed) half-hearted disciples—whom he knows will soon abandon him. He gives them a symbol of his purifying blood by washing their feet. He models for them a life of service and love. He teaches them how to abide in him.

All of this shows us that if we want to make disciples of Jesus, we must invest our time and lives in a similar fashion. *We must be willing to invite people into our lives even when it is inconvenient.*

We give away our time and experiences to others in order that they will grow in their faith in Christ and learn what it looks like to follow Jesus. We invest in others because he invested everything in us! As Paul says,

> "Have this mind among yourselves, which is yours in Christ Jesus, who, though he was in the form of God, did not count equality with God a thing to be grasped, but emptied himself, by taking the form of a servant, being born in the likeness of men. And being found in human form, he humbled himself by becoming obedient to the point of death, even death on a cross." (Phil. 2:5-8)

IMAGINING

One key concept that should not be overlooked in John 14-17 is Jesus's expectation of what his disciples will become after he has departed. In other words, Jesus paints a picture for these disciples about the possibilities that are in store for them if they abide in him. He tells them they will receive the Holy Spirit (14:16, 26); they will be adopted into his family (14:18); they will be one with him and the Father (14:20); they will bear fruit (15:5); they will experience true joy (15:11); persecution will come (15:18); and the gift of a deeper knowledge of the truth (16:12-13). That's just to name a few.

I believe the most overlooked aspect of teaching someone to abide in Christ is this work of "imagining" a different future for them. Life in Christ is full of joy, freedom, and satisfaction.

Knowing and living out your identity in Christ is the work of discipleship, and this leads to re-creation and renewal in the life of a disciple.

We must show others what this life can look like.

As you teach someone to abide in Christ, point to the great and glorious promises that Jesus gives his disciples. *Help them imagine* a different reality—one where King Jesus rules over them as the Servant King, extending grace upon grace to his followers. *Help them see* how this affects their work, their relationships, their marriages, their children's future, or the well-being of their neighborhood and of their city. *Show them* how a good and gracious God can wash the feet of sinners and rescue them from their own selfish ambition and self-hatred.

Discipleship is giving them a new story, with a new plot, and a new Hero, so that they can see the incomparable alternative to their current way of life.

In order to teach others what it means to abide, we must invite them into our lives, investing our time and experiences in them, and imagine a different future for them. My hope is that these simple steps can assist us all in our calling to make disciples of Jesus, through the power of the gospel.

8

WHY DO WE NEGLECT OUR NEIGHBORS?
Alvin L. Reid

I recently spoke at a large, vibrant, multisite church. While speaking about reaching the younger generation, I asked a couple of questions. First, I asked those in each service to raise their hand if they grew up in a Christian home. Without fail, the vast majority raised their hands, most with understandable joy and enthusiasm for their heritage.

Then I asked the second question: "How many of you recall a time in your childhood when your Christian family talked about reaching out to your neighbors with the gospel?" What few were left reticently raised their hands.

Too many of us raise our children in our neighborhoods as if we were atheists. I have asked these two questions in seminary classes, on college campuses, in youth meetings and in large conferences. The response has been the same without exception. For too long, many of us have affirmed a practicing atheism, thinking we can magnify Christ among other Christians while virtually ignoring him when among non-Christians.

Too many of us raise our children in our neighborhoods as if we were atheists.

Can we truly say the gospel lies at the center of our lives and our families, if we raise children from birth to adulthood and they can't recall a conversation about the spiritual need of their neighbors?

WHY DO WE NEGLECT OUR NEIGHBORS?

The reasons for neglecting our neighbors is multifaceted. One reason is tied up with institutional Christianity, which discourages believers from taking initiative apart from a church building. A second reason, and perhaps the most crucial, is this: we have lost wonder over the story and glory of God. Failure to worship God leads to a failed desire to bring our neighbors to worship him with us.

We need to recover the gospel in a way that sets God's glory in the center of all of life. The Bible is unambiguous at this point: the center Scripture is not us, but God, who alone deserves our greatest wonder and all glory. Genesis begins not with us, or even with creation, but with a Creator God who creates for his own glory. John's Gospel does the same, focusing our attention on Christ. Romans does the same. While creation reflects God's glory, he finally and most clearly reveals himself to us in his Son, Jesus. Thus, the central character of the biblical story is the Redeemer who works a story of redemption.

The Bible is taught, even in self-proclaimed Bible-believing churches, in a way that ironically encourages believers to do little that requires sacrifice for the gospel (if you can call investing in your neighbors for Christ a "sacrifice"). We turn the Bible into a collection of moralistic stories (David beat Goliath, so you can beat the giants in your life) in which we are the center and the story is designed to help us. Such an approach gives us many heroes, from Joseph the victimized who overcame abuse to Ruth and Boaz who offer a great encouragement to those seeking romance. In this approach, Jesus matters, but he becomes just a slightly bigger hero than all the rest. Of course, the Bible does offer help with overcoming abuse and in relationships. That help is called *the gospel*.

No, there is one hero in Scripture. But it's okay, I suppose, if we slip up on that at times, because after all, Peter did. At the Transfiguration when Peter saw Jesus with Elijah and Moses, Peter suggested building tents for all three (Lk. 9:33). The Father quickly made it clear that Jesus alone was to be revered: "This is my Son, my Chosen One; listen to him!" (Lk. 9:35). Not even Moses or Elijah compare to Jesus.

We remove Jesus from the central place he deserves when we give lip service to his lordship in church services while neglecting his lordship in our neighborhoods. We need a revolution in our understanding of Jesus. He is the One who initiates, sustains, and will consummate all things. He alone sits on the throne.

FOR US AND OUR NEIGHBORS

What does this have to do with reaching our neighbors? When we consistently hear that the gospel and the Bible as a whole have to do with us, we have no motivation to go to our neighbors, let alone the nations.

But the gospel compels us to reach out locally and globally, from our front porch step to the ends of the earth. The gospel stands at the center, not only of our church life, but the entirety of life. This is why Paul places the gospel at the center of discussions on *giving* (2 Cor. 8), fleeing *sexual temptation* (1 Cor. 6, see especially verse 20), in *marriage* (Eph. 5:25), and as the basis for humility (Phil. 2). In other words, the gospel is for us—for our every sin and every success.

Jesus is the center of history. He is the center of the Bible (Lk. 24:44-48). He is to be the center of our lives. We need his gospel as much as anyone else. We should preach the gospel to ourselves daily, reminding ourselves that life is not about us but about Christ, situating our great depravity under his marvelous grace.

We should preach the gospel to ourselves daily, reminding ourselves that life is not about us but about Christ, situating our great depravity under his marvelous grace.

Why should we care about our neighbors and the nations? We were made as worshippers to glorify God. We are also sent as God's ambassadors to others. Awe of God will lead to witness about God. If the gospel really is good news, then we can't help but share it. Wonder over at God's love for us in Christ compels us to love others enough to tell them about our great Savior.

IN YOUR NEIGHBORHOOD

This is why my family moved into a neighborhood filled with unchurched friends. It's why you've been placed in your neighborhood. Gospel work in our neighborhood has been slow, but we have seen some fruit. Along the way, we're learning to involve our children in care for our neighbors. We've also had the opportunity to take our children all over the world, so they can see the work of the gospel in other places. Although most of us wont have the opportunity to travel the world, we can lead our families in traveling the neighborhood right away! Get out and meet your neighbors. Invite them over for dessert. Make some play dates. Think of ways to serve the neighborhood, and look for opportunities to bring neighbors along towards the wonder of Christ.

The gospel is simply too big, too amazing, too life-changing for us to take it, shut it up in our homes and our church buildings, and live as if we were atheists. The gospel propels us to spread a wonder over God's grace and glory among neighbors and the nations.

What are you waiting for?

9

WHEN IS THE GOSPEL NOT GOOD NEWS?
Stuart McCormack

Sometimes when we share our faith, we can sense the message is not getting through. We can feel that the gospel (the "good news") we have about God's love for the people of the world—highlighted and evidenced through Jesus's life, death, and resurrection—just doesn't resonate as good news with the hearers of the message. How should we respond when the gospel is not "good news"?

If you are anything like me, you'll heartily affirm that the message of the cross is in fact good news. You've experienced it yourself. The gospel has the ability to inwardly transform a person so that the change in their heart spills out into the visible world of the gospel recipient. We believe that the gospel has the power to transform a person from the inside out and that this transformation is indeed good news to those who would receive it by simple faith.

So why do people reject the amazing truth that the gospel is good news? Here are three simple reasons. They are not exhaustive, and I am sure you can think of many more to add to the list.

1. WHEN THEY ARE NOT READY TO RECEIVE THE GOOD NEWS
A wheel chair is an amazing invention! It provides a person the means to move from one place to another often with a good amount of independence. It can enhance the life of a person who has lost the use of their legs. It may raise that person's self-esteem if they feel home-bound or isolated. It can enable them

to be independent and to participate in community or sporting events.

I imagine most of us able-bodied people have not thought about this before. A wheelchair is good news to someone who has lost use of their legs, but to an able-bodied person, it is more than likely just *interesting* news. The difference is found in the *need* for the wheelchair. Most of us do not need a wheelchair. Therefore, we would be unlikely to value information about them.

The gospel is like this. Many people do not receive the gospel simply because they do not yet perceive their *need* for it. This is why it is essential that we continue to preach the whole gospel that without God we are lost. Without Jesus, we are separated from God's love and from God himself. Without the cross, there is no way back to the Father.

Many people simply do not see their need for God. He is outside their list of needs. As preachers and missionaries, we must communicate the gospel at a person's point of *need*. This requires us to get to know people personally. This takes time as we will need to observe and *listen* to those we are sharing the gospel with.

2. WHEN THEIR HEARTS ARE HARD TO THE GOOD NEWS

It is not unusual to come across someone who has hardened themselves to the good news that God loves them. Many people have hardened their hearts to Jesus. This is to be expected in a fallen and broken world. It is well known that when people are hurting, they often put up defenses against being hurt again. These walls surround the heart and are often set up not just against human hurts but also against God who is perceived to be to blame.

The gospel shows us that God reaches out in love, and love is exactly what hurting people need. Think back over your life. When you were hurt by others how did you respond? I know that even with God on my side, I have often taken offense and built mental barriers between myself and others (God included!) in order to "protect" myself. Your friends and family are human like you. They will need the gospel to be incarnated in your lifestyle, actions, and compassion. Not only in your words. A simple response of active love is the first step to softening a persons' heart toward you and the loving God we serve. Small steps and words of *love* are God's good news to those who are hurting.

3. WHEN THEY DON'T SEE ENOUGH EVIDENCE OF THE GOOD NEWS

"But I have shown them so many passages of the Bible that prove who Jesus is and what he has done!" Have you ever felt this way? We might be moved to despair or frustration when our loved ones are not coming to Jesus.

Sharing scriptural support for belief in the gospel is good, but the gospel is not simply about revealing Scripture to people. It is about revealing Jesus (the point of the Scripture) to people. We do this by backing up the verbal gospel message with lives that reflect the truth of the gospel. Our lives need to be bearing the fruit of the gospel that transforms us from the inside out. People need to see the fruit of the Holy Spirit evidenced in the day to day things we do.

It's not going to church that will convince a person that the gospel works (although it might!). It's not just reading your Bible or praying that a person needs to see (although they might!). They need to see how you handle conflict in Godly ways. How you treat your spouse. How you show hospitality unconditionally. How you make yourself available when needs arise. How you speak. How you act. Everything. It is sad but true that often the worst advertisement for the gospel is the carrier of the gospel – me and you. I pray that this would not be the reason our friends, families, neighbors, work colleagues, and enemies reject the gospel. When people don't see the evidence, we need to return to God to soften our hearts to him as we surrender our lives afresh to him.

As we share the gospel, we need to really discern where the hearer is at in life and faith.

Are they oblivious to their need? Help them to see their need. Listen like Jesus.

Are they hurting? Let the gospel be given in love in order to bring healing. Love like Jesus.

Do they lack true evidence that the gospel transforms? Make sure your life matches up to gospel values. Live like Jesus.

10

6 WAYS TO MAKE CHRIST CENTRAL AT HOME
Alvin Reid

Family is, rightfully, one of the most emphasized points in the modern church. Seminars, parenting videos, books, sermon series, and a litany of parachurch ministries focus on the family. While these resources are often good, I believe a vital element has been missing in our approach to parenting.

I often ask my students if they remember their church hosting family-oriented events such as marriage retreats and sermon series. Virtually everyone recalls such a focus. Then I ask, "How many of you recall an emphasis in these events or resources on evangelizing your children or raising them to become Great Commission Christians?" Very few recall such an emphasis.

WHO SHOULD EVANGELIZE OUR CHILDREN?

Nothing matters more to Christian parents than that their children become passionate followers of Christ. Yet, we hardly ever talk about that in the church.

And raising children with a focus on the Great Commission seems about as common as a lemonade stand in the Sahara Desert. I believe this stems, in part, from the institutionalism in our churches, as if presenting Christ to our children was the job of "the church" rather than the parents. Perhaps we also (falsely) assume parents are evangelizing their kids, so we leave it alone.

Being a parent must be the most exciting, frightening, inspiring, upsetting, amazing, routine, joyful and, at times, sorrowful experience in life. I spend a lot of time with youth. Many of them do not have a close relationship with their parents. Many rarely see a family that loves one another. Marriages end in divorce, with fatherless children, and mothers who struggle to get by. It's painful.

How can we avoid this path? How can we cultivate a Christ-centered home?

CHRIST-CENTERED HOME

In Deuteronomy 6, Moses addresses parents and other adults saying: "Listen, Israel: The LORD our God, the LORD is One. Love the LORD your God with all your heart, with all your soul, and with all your strength." Jesus called this the Greatest Commandment. Surely it should be central in any Christian home!

In your decisions as a family, do you seek first to listen to God? Does your family put following what God says above all else? If so, does a passion for the lost have a central part in your home?

Sometimes we miss the centrality of loving God above all when we tell our children to get a good education, good job, but fail to place as much emphasis on hearing and loving God. If God really is this lovely, worthy of our affection and devotion, then do we inspire our children to share the good news about him, to know and enjoy him through Jesus?

We bought our current home with these things in mind. We picked a home that was: first, in a neighborhood of folks not actively churched (and we have great neighbors!); and second, designed to help us focus on being together, namely a large room that can hold a TV and computer. Growing up, our children spent very little time in their rooms because we shared a home, not just a house. Parents who model love for God and family, use their years together to not only love one another but also welcome in the lost. A Christ-centered home is an evangelistic home.

HOW TO MAKE CHRIST CENTRAL AT HOME

Deuteronomy 6:6-9 provides a great outline for parenting:

"These words that I am giving you today are to be in your heart. Repeat them to your children. Talk about them when you sit in your house and when you walk along the road, when you lie down and when you get up. Bind them as a sign on your hand and let them be a symbol on your forehead. Write them on the doorposts of your house and on your gates."

The notion that spiritual training is primarily the job of the church and, in particular, teens the responsibility of a student pastor, *is simply not taught in the Bible.* Deuteronomy 6 puts the responsibility for the spiritual training of a child squarely on the shoulders of parents. We are to instruct them, literally "sharpen the knife," and live truth before them. What does this look like? While it certainly involves active participation in a gospel-centered church, it also includes imparting a longing for the salvation of the neighbors and the nations.

Allow me to breakdown the passage in six practical ways:

1. "These words that I am giving you today are to be in your heart:"

Our children should see us spending time in God's Word, sharing our faith, and demonstrating Christ-like character. They should be aware that the gospel has changed me and is continuing to change me. That includes family worship, family discussions, and family participation in the local church.

2. "Repeat them to your children:"

I should be instructing my children, particularly when young, about the things of God. I should help them see how to live out a biblical worldview, making decisions in all arenas of life from a biblical perspective. I should not raise them to be faithful citizens in a religious subculture, but to see all of creation with biblical eyes.

3. "Talk about them when you sit in your house:"

We do not talk about Jesus to others because we do not talk about him much in our homes. Family mealtime provides a great avenue for talking about Jesus and teaching everything from civility to life lessons. Shared activities with children provide further opportunities for instruction. Research has shown the significant impact of regular family meals. Eat together and invite others to your table.

4. "When you walk along the road:"

The church and the home are not the only places to learn how to live and share Christ. Our activities, from talking to the waitress at the restaurant to being courteous at the mall, help show how to live out our faith rather than compartmentalizing it in the confines of our house and the church building. Simply talking to our neighbors about things that matter help children see the world through missionary eyes. Talk about Jesus in everyday life.

5. "When you lie down and when you get up"

Bedtime, especially for younger children, provides a great time for prayer and instruction in spiritual things. Sit at the end of the bed just a little longer to remind them of spiritual things. Prayer together is important. One *Lifeway* study showed that 88% of Christian families never prayed together ever regularly. We can hardly complain about prayer being taken from the public schools if we are not praying in our Christian homes. Pray morning and evening with your kids.

6. "Bind them as a sign on your hand and let them be a symbol on your forehead. Write them on the doorposts of your house and on your gates:"

I suppose this could include Christian symbols and expressions in our homes, but more importantly, it is vital we incorporate the gospel into the fabric of the family. Is the gospel alive in how we discipline, make family purchases, and respond to suffering? Our interactions with our neighbors should communicate Christ. We need much more than "Christian" conferences and T-shirts. We need Christ applied to the nitty-gritty of life.

Take a moment to consider what role the Great Commission has in your home. How can you and your spouse make changes to cultivate a more Christ-centered home that, not only evangelizes your children but also your neighbors? The greatest missionary force in America today sleeps in our bedrooms. May we lead, teach, and equip them well.

11

DISCIPLESHIP THROUGH FAMILY WORSHIP
Luma Simms

Scripture does not give us an imperative for family worship. This is important to say at the outset so that we are not laying down "sanctification markers" for each other. Having said that, however, we still need to acknowledge that God's Word does command us to teach our children how to love the Lord (Deut. 6) and train them in his discipline and instruction (Eph. 6:4).

PRINCIPLES AND METHODS
Before looking at family worship, it is important to discuss the Bible's principles that we are to take and wisely apply in our particular situation. We should not do this just to go along with the more "sanctified" crowd. No, we are to be realistic about ourselves, our children, our own family culture, and our strengths and weaknesses. Then, we should prayerfully and wisely make household decisions. So whether in education, entertainment, clothing styles, family activities, and so on, we look to Scripture for liberties and boundaries to make thoughtful, prayerful choices.

Sometimes, we may find that the choice we made doesn't fit with our individual family, and we should adjust. Either way, when Scripture gives us principles, we should not use our particular application as a measuring rod for other people's devotion to Christ, nor are we to hold it up as the only *godly* way of living out a particular biblical principle. We need to give each other grace to execute these principles differently in the context of our individual families. This is one of the differences between principles and methods.

FAMILY WORSHIP

I've prayed for my children throughout pregnancy, during delivery, and over them as babies. Even when we were nominal Christians, we prayed with our children before bed. But I remember distinctly the first time I saw what is known as "family worship." We had just moved into a new neighborhood and began attending a small Reformed church when a dear family took us under their wing and began mentoring us. They invited us into their home, and we got to see first-hand a family living the life of faithful Christians.

I was a green-behind-the-ears stay-at-home mom, desiring to learn what this new role—which I had been kicking against and hoping to avoid—really looked like day in and day out. Even though I had just delivered our third child we felt new in our roles because we had at that same time decided to eschew feminism, careerism, and egalitarianism for "the traditional biblical model," if such a thing was possible.

This family at the time was going through Starr Meade's *Training Hearts, Teaching Minds*. Their love for each other and the responsiveness of the children to the parents was evident. And so we promptly bought the same book, which is a family devotional based on the *Westminster Shorter Catechism*. After a few months, our mentor family moved away, but we kept on going with our family worship. We did different books through different seasons. But things kept escalating until we arrived at the point where my husband wrote a family liturgy that we would recite—a liturgy that might be beautiful if done correctly in a church but not fit for family worship. In our zeal for "godliness," we crushed our children under a weight masquerading as family worship.

TOOLS OF DISCIPLESHIP

Family worship is a tool, and if the parents are tethered to the gospel, it can be a wonderful discipleship tool in the home. However, if this tool is not used wisely, it can become a joyless burden to the children. Discernment is required. We should probably think through a few guiding principles as we seek to use the tool of family worship in our homes.

1. A Merciful Perspective

We need to remember to be merciful to our children in the area of family worship. Many Christian parents love their children and desire them to grow into Christ followers. This is as it should be, and I praise God for it. But with this comes a temptation that we should be aware of and work to keep in check. We can be *so* driven by our desires to see our kids saved and sanctified we forget how God deals with us as *his* children. I think it is helpful to not only think of ourselves as parents but as children—children of our heavenly Father. If we keep this thought at the forefront of our parenting, it will drive us to be more mindful of their perspective or *frame*.

> As a father shows compassion to his children, so the Lord shows compassion to those who fear him. For he knows our *frame*; he remembers that we are dust. (Ps. 103:13–14)

In this Psalm, God is compared to a father who shows compassion on his children. If we are not characterized by compassion to our children, this should cause us to do a 180-degree turn! Scrolling up to verse 8, we are told, "The Lord is merciful and gracious, slow to anger and abounding in steadfast love. He will not always chide, nor will he keep his anger forever. He does not deal with us according to our sins, nor repay us according to our iniquities."

Do we give our children this kind of bountiful grace or do we call them on the carpet for every sin? Do we spend our time chiding them for their wriggly bottoms during family worship or do we adjust our expectations of these little souls remembering our own wriggly bottoms when the Lord is trying to teach us something? Psalm 130:3 says, "If you, O Lord, should mark iniquities, O Lord, who could stand? But with you there is forgiveness, that you may be feared."

2. Acts of Gentleness

Let us take our parenting cues from our heavenly Father. Does your family have a two year old? Well, maybe he gets his own bedtime prayer and you wait until that little person is asleep instead of forcing a tired toddler to sit still in the lap to "participate" in family worship. A time of day when everyone is excited to be together and involved would be a good time to harness to use for building your children in the Lord (e.g. meal time, prayer time right before bed when most children tend to be more open and willing to be gently shepherded).

Think back to how long-suffering your heavenly Father has been with you. How many of your sins has he forgiven? How long has it taken you to get to where you are right now and how much more time will it take to be formed into the image of Christ? This should correct our expectations of our children and help us enact gentle kindness and long-suffering patience toward them as we use the tool of family worship in our home.

3. Relentless Prayer

Next, we must remember that family worship is only *one* tool, not the *only* tool, that the Lord can and will use in the life of your child. Don't let it be the end-all and be-all, which was my temptation and stumbling block. Our heavenly Father is so creative. Every day I am surprised at the manifold ways he works on my children's hearts.

The most potent tool for discipling and reaching the heart of your children is—shocker!—prayer. No "family this" or "family that" will ever have the power to transform the lives of the members of the family like prayer in the name of Jesus. Let us be like the widow who was relentless and persistent, who wouldn't stop going to the judge (Lk. 18:1–8). Let us day and night bombard Heaven with prayers for, and often with, our children.

PUTTING WORSHIP BACK IN FAMILY WORSHIP

Having said all this, I do want to note that the Lord does indeed use the methods of family worship. I certainly don't want to discount that, I just want to put it in its proper place. Family worship should not occupy the center. Jesus does. Family worship is a tool that I personally love and believe can bring depth to the spiritual life of a family, when used wisely.

In our case, we now use three different gospel-centered books for family worship. We have five children of varying ages. For us, we needed gospel-focused books that would work in a family that has kids of all ages. So we rotate between using *The Jesus Storybook Bible* by Sally-Lloyd Jones, *The Gospel Story Bible* by Marty Machowski, and *Long Story Short* also by Marty Machowski.

We are not perfectionists about these books. Sometimes we do one lesson or story. Other times we do more. We give the kids who can read the Bible readings to read to the family. We put the baby to bed first so he isn't a distraction and so we're not spending all our time trying to keep him still.

We also allow the children to choose what they want to pray for. Usually the older ones will pray for global saints and churches, the middle prays for church family members on the church prayer calendar, and our little guy just loves to pray for his baby brother.

Now, this is just an example of our method. Don't feel compelled to go follow it. Pray and consider the frame of your children. Maybe what is best for right now is a short prayer in the morning with a verse or something from *The Jesus Storybook Bible*. There was a time when teaching and reciting the Children's Catechism was fruitful for us, and a time when it was good for us to look elsewhere. Explore different options and don't get caught in that harsh place where the perfect becomes the enemy of the good. Don't be too disappointed if something doesn't work out, keep trying.

Above all, remember that the goal of any of these discipleship tools is to draw that little person's (or big person's) soul to Jesus Christ. We don't need to prove our theological prowess to our children, we just need to show them the same kind of love Jesus shows us.

12

HOW KIDS LEARN TO FOLLOW JESUS
Seth McBee

One of the common questions I see is, "What about kids? How do you have time to disciple your children during all this mission stuff and what does it look like?"

I have three kids, I own a business, I am an elder in a church, I preach, and I participate as an executive team member of the GCM Collective. Not to mention, I coach leaders around the world and travel for speaking and training events. How do I have time? I learned early on, from my brothers at Soma Communities, that I only have one life, and that mission has to be part of my everyday life, not some other life that I need to live. I don't have time to get into all of that teaching, but it transformed how I see mission and discipleship. Needless to say, I've decided to serve and leverage my life as much as I can. I'm busy and you are probably busy, too. So how can we disciple kids in the midst of such hectic community and mission-filled lives?

HOLISTIC DISCIPLESHIP
What is the goal of children's discipleship? We're not just trying to teach them stuff, right? See, the goal is not that our children will merely know the right answers on their Bible college theological entry exam or in Sunday school. We certainly want them to know God and understand the gospel in their minds. But, discipleship cannot stop at intellectual assent of biblical truths; it must penetrate their hearts, too.

In the same way, the goal is not for children discipleship cannot stop at their hearts, but must be evidenced in their lives. Certainly our children's discipleship is not only about getting them to behave and use proper manners. The Bible speaks to parenting and disciple-making more holistically than this:

> You shall therefore lay up these words of mine in your heart and in your soul, and you shall bind them as a sign on your hand, and they shall be as frontlets between your eyes. You shall teach them to your children, talking of them when you are sitting in your house, and when you are walking by the way, and when you lie down, and when you rise. You shall write them on the doorposts of your house and on your gates. (Deut. 11:18-20)

This passage tells us two fundamental principles in parenting. One, discipleship is for the head, heart, and hand. We are to teach our children to know the gospel, believe the gospel, and obey the gospel. Two, the discipleship process is happening all the time, in everyday life. Every moment of the day is a chance to speak, teach, and demonstrate the gospel. My aim with this article is to offer some easy handles and ideas for parents to obediently live Deuteronomy 11 with their kids.

HEAD

We want our kids to know theology. We want them to know who God is, what God has done, who we are, and how we should live. The issue is often that our kids get bored with this subject. Memorize this verse, sit here for Sunday school, listen to mommy and daddy read from the Bible. None of those things are bad, but what if we could do this in ways that they'd actually love and look forward to? Consider these ideas:

First, watch your kids' favorite TV shows with them. At the end, discuss the ways the characters are living out their identity, how are their lives looking like Jesus, how are their lives showing who/what they are trusting. For my kids, it's *Phineas and Ferb*. We sit down and watch it, then discuss. The night before I wrote this, we spoke about servanthood, identity, idols, fears, anxiety, the image of God, etc. After we discussed, we prayed as a family for very specific things that we discussed. Guess what the kids are always asking to do? "Daddy, can we do *Phineas and Ferb* and theology?" They desire to learn because it is something they enjoy.

Second, teach them from material they will enjoy and let them teach and dialogue through it. I personally use two resources: *The Jesus Story Book Bible* and *The Story of God for Kids*. When we read, I am always asking questions to get their insight. These resources are great because there are pictures and questions that get the kids involved; they can't just sit there and listen. I also allow my ten-year-old to lead so he can learn what it looks like to lead and create discussion. In this, I am able to disciple him in what it looks like to lead by allowing him to do it himself.

HEART

Not only do we want our children to learn theology and mission through teaching, but we want them to believe it and know it in their hearts. We want it to go from information to transformation. Know this: there will be times that it sails over their heads. We will articulate the gospel in eloquent ways and they will have no reaction. But we have to be faithful. Find out how to affect their heart by seeking the Spirit and continue to do it, even if you don't get the reaction you were hoping for. Here are some ways it has worked for me:

First, discipline like you believe the gospel. I learned this from John Piper some years ago. He simply asked, "Does your discipline mirror grace and the gospel or legalism?" My kids never know when they are going to be punished for a sin. I try to sit them down after they have sinned and walk through grace and mercy and the effects of sin. We get to the heart of the issue of their sin, instead of just saying, "Stop that!" There are times when they are not punished for their sin, and we speak a lot about grace. There are also times when their sin causes natural consequences. For example, they might leave a favorite toy outside when they were supposed to bring it inside and it gets ruined. When this happens, we merely point out the consequence and pray together for forgiveness and reconciliation. When you spend time demonstrating in discipline what grace, the gospel and reconciliation looks like, it hits the heart.

Second, demonstrate that you believe the gospel. I got this idea from my buddy Caesar. One of the discipleship issues we had with our older child had to do with his behavior while he was playing outside. We decided that if he was having issues playing outside, he would have to come inside or face punishment. The punishment was to sit on the wall for 20 minutes. Lots of fun. Instead, when the time came for him to receive his punishment, I told him I'd take it for him. We talked about Jesus and the good news and how he has done this for us. This sounded great, but he listened, and then ran back outside like nothing happened. I still do this, because I think at some point, it will sink in. But you have to know: they are kids and they won't always react in the ways you were hoping. Don't give up.

Third, when you see your child do something that reminds you of Jesus, tell them and praise them for it. When they see how their actions depict God's character, it really freaks them out. One of my kids recently asked, "God works through me to show who he is?" It really hit him. Our kids need to hear about God, not only when they are doing things that are disappointing, but also when they are showing the fruit of the Spirit. Recently, another of my kids came up and told me that his little brother made him lunch for school. He was stoked! I told him, "Caleb, where do you think he learned that?" He replied, "God?" I said, "He learned it from you as you have been serving him. And you learned it from God as Jesus served and serves you. You have been showing your brother Jesus. Isn't it amazing that he does those things he sees in you as you show him Jesus?"

Finally, continue to remind them they are loved by God and you, no matter what. We do this in both their sin and in their praise. We want them to continually know that God loves regardless of their actions. Their identity and acceptance is not wrapped up in what they do, but in who God is and what he does. I do this when they do something that requires discipline and I do this when they show off who God is.

HANDS

Not only do our kids need to know about God in their head, and know what he's done in their heart, but they also need to work this out as disciples and missionaries. We have to know and communicate that our children are not missionaries only when they get older—they are missionaries now. Here are some ideas:

First, involve your kids in the mission. Rarely do we do things that don't involve our kids. When we do events, most of the time it is with families. I want my kids to see that it is totally normal to be around those who don't believe like us, and show them what it looks like to hang out with them. I don't want them to ever think that our job is to do things so we'll get something in return. We merely show others what God is like. We plant, we water, but God causes the growth. The best way to do this is to model it for them in life-on-life. So, at neighborhood barbecues or neighborhood breakfasts, they have jobs before and after. We talk about why we are doing these, what their thoughts are, and their struggles with it. They get to walk this out and deal with the consequences of following Jesus: when their toys get broken, when they have to clean up after others, etc. When all this happens, we get to talk about what it means to serve and show off Jesus without expecting anything in return.

Second, make your house the "hang-out-house." Our kids know that they can always have friends over for dinner or slumber parties. Because of this, they are actively sharing their lives with those around us. They see what it means to have an open home, to be hospitable, to believe that our possessions are God's and not ours. They also know that to open our home means there will sometimes be kids they don't want to play with, but we open our home anyway. We love our enemies, we don't hate them or shun them. The more you allow your kids to have people over and just hang out and play, the more they will be able to understand mission in the everyday.

Third, invite their friends and parents out to your activities. Recently, I took my boys to a movie and dinner, so I asked them who they wanted to bring. I then invited their friends and their family to go out with us. Again, this is simple. Their friends and families came and hung out. We were already going to do it, why not do it with others? This doesn't mean we eat dinner and ask the other dad, "You see the bread on your kid's plate? That reminds of when Jesus said he was the bread of life." Treat them well, be their friend, and show your kids what it looks like to be hospitable toward others in all areas of life.

Finally, ask your children what charity they'd like to help on their birthday. We have done this with both our older kids. We tell them, "Mom and Dad will buy you a gift, and so will your grandparents, but what if we had your friends bring something for a charity?" We have had food drives, blanket drives, and more for one of our missional communities that helps the homeless in our town. Our kids actually love doing this! They get to help others and participate in serving.

NORMAL LIFE WITH INTENTIONALITY

I know these things aren't earth-shattering ideas. They are simple, everyday activities. That's the point. We don't need some program to raise our children for us; we can do this in normal, everyday life. Through this, our kids will understand what following Jesus looks like and will hopefully desire to do it, too. Some days are better than others, some things work better than others. You know your family. Try different ideas. A simple way to start is just to look at your schedule with your family and start asking, how can we be more intentional with these things we are already doing so our children can better understand who God is, what he has done, who he has made us? What can we do to holistically disciple our children, their head, heart, and hands?

What if *your* parents taught you about God while watching cartoons? Pretty cool parents, pretty fun way to learn theology.

13

5 WAYS TO GRACE YOUR WORKPLACE
Nick Abraham

I currently work in a "secular" job for a Fortune 500 company. I put the word *secular* in quotes because it's a common misconception that there is such a thing as secular work. When we think this way, we may be tempted to view pastors or clergy as the only people that do any type of ministry work. As Paul reminds us in Ephesians 4, this is not the case.

Also, I mention that I am Christian because according to my faith in Christ, I am to be a certain kind of employee, which is a part of my overall calling to be a certain kind of citizen and a certain kind of person. The Christian faith calls us to be a certain kind of people, a distinct people. We become a people set apart to live as Christ calls us to live as the Holy Spirit lives in and through us. As the apostle Peter tells us, "But you are a chosen race, a royal priesthood, a holy nation, a people for his own possession, that you may proclaim the excellencies of him who called you out of darkness into his marvelous light" (1 Pt. 2:9). And we are called to be that distinct and chosen people in the world, including our jobs.

Before working at my present job, I was a cook for five years at an Italian restaurant. If you have worked in the restaurant industry, you know that it can draw interesting and diverse employees. During that time, I became a Christian. I never thought that I would be in a more challenging work atmosphere to share and live out my faith. While my current work atmosphere is really nothing like the restaurant, I have found an entirely new set of challenges in living out my faith at work. The truth is, there are always challenges to carrying the gospel message in a fallen world, regardless of the context.

EVERY GOOD ENDEAVOR

The corporate world presents a unique veneer of professionalism, ethics, and propriety. The reality is that the day-to-day in a corporate job can be quite challenging. There are a myriad of moral conundrums that come up in an office. We are faced with temptations to gossip and engage in malicious chatter when others aren't around. We are faced with struggles involving the opposite sex. We are broken people, and being in the workplace does not make that brokenness go away until we get home.

As a Christian, my integrity is often challenged by the situations in which I am placed. But beyond the personal struggles, I want to reflect the gospel well. My co-workers need to see whether or not their perception of Christianity holds up. It doesn't matter if their perspective of Christianity is correct or not; they will judge for themselves based on what they know. If I am given the privilege and permission to share what I believe—and most importantly who Jesus is—I have an opportunity to shape their outlook on Christianity.

Living out the gospel at work is not some add-on to the Christian life that we can choose if we want; it's a realization of the fullness of the Christian life. Being in Christ is meant to encompass all of our lives. The workplace is a prime opportunity to do just that.

Recently, a friend gave me Tim Keller's book, *Every Good Endeavor*. As he usually does, Keller wonderfully connected work and faith in my own heart. So, I had a conversation with my manager about the book and asked if I could have an optional meeting during lunch with anyone in the department that would like to read together. It was approved, and we had seven people in our group. We met every week to discuss a chapter. The discussions were great, and it was the first time that some of them thought about connecting faith and work.

Christian, your job is a ministry, plain and simple. God planted you in your current job for a particular reason. "And we know that for those who love God all things work together for good, for those who are called according to his purpose" (Rom. 8:28). The apostle Paul is telling us here that God is working out his will in the lives of his people. And at the cross, Jesus has freed us from making our work about us and has given us the gospel to revel in and tell others about.

REPRESENTING WELL

So, how do we represent the gospel well in the workplace? Here are a five ways to grace your workplace:

1. Be Bold but Smart

We can and must think on Paul's boldness before Felix in Acts 24, or Jesus's words on being brought before governors and kings in Matthew 10. Just because we are at work does not mean we are no longer a disciple of Jesus. We are never exempt from the call on our lives to make much of him. However, we must be smart and keep in mind passages like 1 Peter 2:13: "Be subject for the Lord's sake to every human institution." At work, we are subject to our bosses and to the leader or leaders of the company. So be bold, but keep in mind where you are.

2. Take Risks

I realize this somewhat contradicts the last point, but the Christian life rests in a tension between risk and prudence. (For this point, I really should tell you to just go listen to anything that John Piper says about risk.) Practically though, take steps in work friendships to bring up Jesus. I am a relational evangelist, meaning I like to establish some type of friendship and then bring up Jesus. I am rarely the "can I tell you about Jesus?" guy. My weakness is to never actually bring up Jesus, or to do so in overly-softened ways. Risk a friendship, risk a promotion, risk not "fitting in," or maybe even risk your job if God would call you to that. Of course, we don't want to be reckless just for the sake of being reckless. Again, find that tension.

3. Pray for Your Enemies

There will be people who do not like you for any number of reasons. Make it a practice to pray for the people that don't seem to like you, who you don't really get along with, or who just always seem to have something snarky to say to or about you. This is incredibly hard, which is why you need to rely on the Spirit in this. You will also discover God ministering to you even as you pray. Pray for them, for their families, for their kids. Most importantly, pray for their relationship with Jesus.

4. Use Your Gift(s)

I am a teacher/pastor type. I usually go into a teaching or pastoral mode at some point during my faith encounters with co-workers. The church is still the church both gathered and scattered. While at work we continue to be part of the church scattered, and in the church we are called to use our gifts to build up the body. Pray about and find a way to use your gift(s). Start a Bible study, start a prayer group, take people's prayer requests and pray for them, give of your time, talents, or treasures to those in need. Be encouraging and impart godly wisdom. Do whatever it takes to be a reconciling minister of the gospel (2 Cor. 5:18-20).

5. Work Hard

Be on time, care about your job, follow the rules, get your work done, and help others. Non-believers can be good employees, too. What makes us different is really captured in the household codes contained in many of the epistles. "Servants, be subject to your masters with all respect, not only to the good and gentle but also to the unjust" (1 Pt. 2:18). The gospel shapes this. We should be that "good" employee no matter who we work for, what the conditions are, and/or whether we like the job. It is sharing in these sufferings of Christ, light they may be, that we can make much of Christ by working hard with integrity. Never let laziness or grumbling be your calling card. Let the gospel destroy your pride and fill you with humility.

May God bless us as we seek to serve and make much of Christ in all areas of our lives.

To them God chose to make known how great among the Gentiles are the riches of the glory of this mystery, which is Christ in you, the hope of glory. Him we proclaim, warning everyone and teaching everyone with all wisdom, that we may present everyone mature in Christ. For this I toil, struggling with all his energy that he powerfully works within me. (Col. 1:27-29)

MATURE
DISCIPLES

14

FACING OUR IDENTITY ISSUES
Jonathan K. Dodson

I sat in my office sulking. My day had been demanding. My week tiresome. My month was an all-out marathon, minus the cheering crowd.

Pastoring eternal souls, preaching week after week, leading leaders, and living an outwardly-focused life is demanding enough, but occasionally the demands pile higher. As a pastor, I am a sinner that counsels sinners. This means that, despite our common hope in the gospel, there are times that I fail to apply my own counsel to my own soul. It means that I'm not enough for *one* disciple, much less a whole church.

The past couple of weeks had been one of those "pile-up" weeks. More counseling, more speaking, more demands. Add to the stack a particular situation that was, shall we say, extreme? The inbox had hate mail and church slander waiting for me. I had to watch self-destructive behavior dismantle a person whom I had poured a lot of life into.

Exhausted, I thought, "No one understands what it's like to be a pastor. "I deserve better treatment than this, after all I've done. Why can't I have better circumstances?" I was emotionally drained.

In hope, I turned to Chuck Palahniuk—author of *Choke, Snuff,* and *Fight Club*—for help.

SPLIT IDENTITY

Chuck Palahniuk writes sketchy fiction that challenges the prevailing norms for identity in our culture. His book *Fight Club* exposes misplaced identity through the central characters: The Narrator (played by Edward Norton in the movie version) and Tyler Durden (played by Brad Pitt). Durden starts underground fighting clubs where men show up after hours to fight barechested and barefoot.

In the now famous scene from *Fight Club* the movie, Durden gives a speech that clarifies just what kind of war we should be fighting:

> We are the middle children of history, man. No purpose or place. We have no great war, or great depression. Our great war is a spiritual war. Our great depression is our lives. We've all been raised by television to believe that one day we'll all be millionaires and movie gods and rock stars—but we won't.

Our great war is a spiritual war. But what kind of spiritual war?

The spiritual war, according to Chuck, is to ground your identity in *reality* not in the American Dream. This is precisely what Edward Norton struggles to do. It was what I was struggling to do. Norton wants to be sexier and cooler than he actually is. He wants to be Brad Pitt, and he wants it so badly that he creates an alter-ego called Tyler Durden, who starts Fight Clubs and lives like a rock god. He believes the lie that ubermasculinity and rock star living will give his life meaning, a greater sense of identity. So he creates Tyler Durden *in his mind*. You might say he has "identity issues," but he's not the only one.

IDENTITY-OF-THE-MOMENT

We all have identity issues. Many of us have created an alter ego. It's more subtle than Norton's, but it's an alter ego nonetheless.

This alternate personality contends for your identity. It pulls at your heart, your longings. It tells you that if you were just a little more like this or that, then you'd be somebody. If you were better looking, if you were more successful, if you were married, if you were more spiritual, if you had more of a following on Twitter or Facebook, then you'd be somebody.

How do you detect your alter ego? Where do your thoughts drift when you have down time? What do you daydream about? Follow your thoughts, your dreams, your calendar and you will quickly find your alter ego. In an interview with *Paste Magazine*, Chuck Palahniuk shares where part of his vision for *Fight Club* came from. He notes that the fighting in *Fight Club* was more about:

> people need[ing] a consensual forum in which to express themselves and to exhaust their pent up anxiety, and also to test themselves and kind of *destroy their identity-of-the-moment, so that they can move on to a better, stronger identity*

His book really is about identity—destroying the unwanted identity-of-the-moment (alter ego) and finding a better, stronger identity. This is what's at stake in our discipleship, every, single, day. A better identity.

RECOVERING IDENTITY IN CHRIST

What if we became adept at identifying our identity-of the-moment, the egos and images we slip into for meaning and worth? What if we were quick to confess those to friends and community? Just think what could happen if you consistently saw through your sin to your identity-of-the-moment, and turned to Christ for true identity. It could be life-changing! Here are a few tips that have helped me recover identity in Christ in my insane moments:

First, reflect on identity-of-the-moment.
I look for the sinful patterns in my life and trace them back to this. For instance, my sin was *sulking* and my false identity was

victim. I try to ask myself the hard questions, but often I need others to do that for me. Our self-image is as accurate as a carnival mirror, says Paul Tripp. We need good questions to straighten out our self-perception. We need to ask questions. "What are you longing for most right now?" "Why are your emotions so extreme?" Check out David Powlison's helpful "X-ray Questions" for more on this (*Seeing with New Eyes*, 132-40).

Second, look for symptoms.
Mine was sulking. Sulkers are sour because they focus on how they've been mistreated. They see themselves as victims—their identity-of-the-moment. Complaining is a sure sign that my victim identity is creeping in. "Can you believe they did that? There's no way I deserve that." Complaining can quickly turn to ripping on people. If we're not careful, best friends and spouses will end up colluding with us for other's verbal demise. "Venting" is an extreme expression of victim identity. We need a better identity in that moment.

Third, reject this alter identity.
Once I detect my sin/identity issue, I try to reject it. Confession to God is the first step. "Lord, I am finding my worth in my wallowing, in being pitied, and I'm not trusting your providence. I don't believe that these circumstances are a kindness from you appointed to lure me deeper into you. I confess *and I receive* forgiveness and cleansing" (see 1 Jn. 1:9). When we confess our sin, we reject our false, alter identity. It's the first step toward gospel sanity, shaking off the delusions of sin, and returning to the grandeur of grace.

Finally, return to Christ.
Returning to Jesus for gospel identity instead of an identity-of-the-moment is the most difficult *and* important part of being a disciple. Robert Murray McCheyene said: "For every look at sin, look ten times at Christ." How does Christ offer you a better identity than the false identity? My sin was sulking and my identity was *victim*. In 2 Peter 1:3, I'm reminded that my identity is godly; I'm a partaker of the divine nature. I was sulking in

ungodliness because I thought I deserved better circumstances. I felt weak. This time I turned to Peter the Apostle, not Chuck Palahniuk.

Peter reminded me that we have "divine power granted to us for life and godliness." This Scripture reminded me of my identity—godly—but it does not stop there. It also offers a Savior to trust, a counter-promise of *divine* power necessary to live a godly life rather than a sulking life. What a relief! Our identity is godly, and our promise is divine power for godliness.

IDENTITY-IN-COMMUNITY

Interestingly, some of the material for Palahniuk's book came from his experience in hospice patient therapy. During one Christmas, he picked a paper ornament off of a church Christmas tree, the kind that obligates you to a good deed like buying a gift for an underprivileged child. His ornament called him to give hospice patients a ride to their therapy sessions. As he sat through some of these sessions, he reported that:

> I started to recognize that, in a way, 12-step groups, recovery groups, support groups were becoming the new kind of church of our time—a place where people will go and confess their very worst aspects of their lives and *seek redemption and community with other people* in the way that *people used to go to church* and sort of present their worst selves in confession and then celebrate communion and then go home for another week.

This need for redemption and community is what provoked some Chuck's themes in *Fight Club*. It's time the church took those things back. It's time we became a community that confesses the worst part of our lives to one another, *but doesn't stop there*. We need more than confession, more than identity-of-the-moment exposure. We need sanity, to return to our true selves in Christ, in community. We need people who will point us to the redemption that is in Jesus. People that won't let us sulk for too long, people who will reminds us that our identity isn't victim. It is son or daughter of the Living God, "partakers of the divine nature," godly ones. I've traced out one way we can do this in *Gospel-Centered Discipleship*, a community-based, gospel-centered approach to following Jesus. However you do it, make a habit of exposing false identities and re-grounding true identity in Christ.

15

REFLECT CHRIST, DEFLECT SATAN
Brandon D. Smith

Paul's story is well documented. He was a killer of Christians and an adamant opponent of their faith (Acts 8:1-3). Later, as a man saved by God's grace, he constantly urged believers to turn away from their old lives and to press into their new natures in Christ, just as he did. He didn't harp on rules and regulations, but rather exhorted them to look to Christ for their reason for living. And as a hate-monger transformed into a humble servant, Paul knew the benefit of receiving and offering Christ's compassion.

Few passages in the New Testament describe the character of Christ as a weapon against Satan's work as clearly as Ephesians 4:25-32. In this passage, Paul makes a very clear assertion to believers: Christians are freed through the sacrifice of Christ, by the power of the Spirit, to reflect him and deflect Satan.

SPEAK TRUTH (V. 25)
Paul states, "Therefore, having put away falsehood, let each one of you speak the truth with his neighbor, for we are members one of another." In short, he is telling his audience to be honest with one another. He does not issue this warning against lying in order to be seen as righteous to outsiders or to prevent themselves from consequences later on; rather, Paul says that Christians should speak the truth because they are one body.

The word for "members" in the Greek, *mele*, literally means "a bodily organ or limb," giving the metaphor that Christians are plainly, not just figuratively, connected as flesh and bone members of a body. It is indispensable for believers to understand that, in a sense, they should treat each other how they themselves want to be treated. If a believer lies to a brother, he is simply sinning against every other Christian and, essentially, himself. Paul carries this thought from verse 24 in which he tells believers to "put on the new self, created after the likeness of God in true righteousness and holiness." Although Christians will always struggle with Satan's temptation to speak falsely until the moment of death, they become new creations in Christ with the ability to walk in a manner that reflects the likeness of God himself.

CONTROL ANGER (VV. 26-27)

The passage continues, expanding on the statements made in previous verses, saying, "Be angry and do not sin; do not let the sun go down on your anger, and give no opportunity to the devil." These two verses combine to explain that such characteristics belong to the devil and not to God. Anger in and of itself is not a sin when exercised appropriately. Even Christ, who did not sin (2 Cor. 5:21; Heb. 4:15), was angry (without sinning) as he rebuked the "money-changers" in the temple (Matt. 21:12-13). When Christians act in such a way that they are representing Satan's lies and not Christ's model, they are in danger of, or already participating in, sin. Francis Foulkes clarifies, "The Christian must be sure that his anger is that of righteous indignation, and not just an expression of personal provocation or wounded pride. It must have no sinful motives, nor be allowed to lead to sin in any way."

Christians are a new creation with a new attitude and a new power to overcome the traps of Satan. Given the opportunity to hold a grudge, the Christian must turn away from their anger and forgive immediately. If "the sun goes down" on a person's anger, it will continually eat them alive, just as Satan has planned. Satan is a powerful trickster, looking for and providing any avenue for a person to give into temptation and give him a place to work. The gospel affords the opportunity to escape such traps.

BE GENEROUS (V. 28)

For the Christian, there is a new outlook on the idea of giving and receiving: "Let the thief no longer steal, but rather let him labor, doing honest work with his own hands, so that he may have something to share with anyone in need." Once given this new life in Christ, a person is called to view their possessions differently. Once a thief himself, the new believer must now work honestly for their income and turn it into a gift.

One only needs to look at the life and ministry of Jesus to see that servanthood is the paramount trait of a holy person. Christ was and is God who stepped into human history and lived a perfect, sinless life. As an eternal king, he had no true reason to be humble or to serve anyone, but he did. He gave all of himself in order that Christians might have a life more than they ever imagined (Jn. 10:10-11). Though Satan makes selfishness appealing, the humble character of Christ cannot be overlooked by anyone seeking to model themselves after him. Dishonest gain may often be the easy route to travel, but believers are commissioned to take the road less traveled.

SHOW GRACE (V. 29)

"Let no corrupting talk come out of your mouths, but only such as is good for building up, as fits the occasion, that it may give grace to those who hear." Here, believers are told not to speak in such a way that someone will be hurt or pushed away by their words. Satan will use biting words to attempt to destroy not only the body of Christ, but relationships they have with outsiders.

Society often judges Christians based upon their actions. The world is not merely looking for a show, but an authentic lifestyle that promotes goodness. While it is rather easy for the Christian to settle into moralistic behavior modification in order to attempt at pleasing Christ and appearing righteous to those around him, the new man cannot stop there; he must act in sincere concern for those looking to him for answers on Christ.

Any person can modify behavior, but a true disciple of Christ lives with a transformed heart that sees other human beings as lost souls in need of Christ's redemption. Satan will try to distract believers from the Great Commission, but this must be fought against. There is no escaping the call to love others as Christ does.

DO NOT GRIEVE THE SPIRIT (V. 30)

Paul advises Christians: "Do not grieve the Holy Spirit of God, by whom you were sealed for the day of redemption." This is a simple caution with huge implications. When sinning, one must remember that their sin is not only damaging to others; it's an affront to God.

The Holy Spirit is God, the third person of the Trinity. The Holy Spirit may sometimes be under appreciated and overlooked by many Christians, but the he is the actual person of God dwelling within the Christian. As the Holy Spirit dwells in the believer, he is rightly and justly saddened and angered by the direct disregard for his holy standard. When the Christian sins, it is not to be forgotten that the holy and righteous God of the universe takes full notice. God is not a distant being, floating in the outskirts of creation; God is an active and living being dwelling in and standing beside each person every day of their existence with full knowledge of their transgressions against him. John Calvin once exhorted Christians to "endeavor that the Holy Spirit may dwell cheerfully within you, as in a pleasant and joyful dwelling, and give him no occasion for grief."

Christians should give thanks for the seal of redemption (Eph. 1:13-14) given to them by God through Christ on the Roman cross. It is in him and him alone that the old man dies and the new man is raised to new life. This new life holds the promise of eternal liberation, while Satan only offers bondage and destruction.

ATTITUDE MATTERS (V. 31)

Paul collects all wrong attitudes together in one verse, telling his audience to "let all bitterness and wrath and anger and clamor and slander be put away from you, along with all malice." Though surely a problem in the church that Paul is writing to, any and all Christians can attest to struggling with these very things. As a Christian, this desire does not simply disappear on the day of new life. There is still constant battle within the soul of a Christian to do what is right and holy when Satan's temptation seems to be the correct—or at least easier— way to handle the negative situation.

The simple response for the Christian is to ignore a person who wrongs them by "turning the other cheek." This is true and virtuous. However, with the power of the Holy Spirit within the believer, there is far more power over sin than merely walking away or pretending that an offense didn't occur. A new creation in Christ has every resource imaginable to actively pursue radical forgiveness and grace. The act of loving an enemy is far and above the call of mere forgiveness. After all, even a non-believer with no supernatural power at all can turn away from a person who insults, attacks, or demeans them. God promises something better; he promises "a way of escape" for believers (1 Cor. 10:13).

BE KIND AND FORGIVING (V. 32)

Paul concludes the passage with this statement: "Be kind to one another, tenderhearted, forgiving one another, as God in Christ forgave you." Believers are called to such a lifestyle because they are new creations with a new heart, first forgiven by God so that they may show grace to the world. The selfish Christian is a contradiction; no one set free from sin can simultaneously be a captive to it. Paul is entirely clear in verse 24 that there is no such thing as a Christian that lives as he once did.

A major facet of the gospel is that having the inclination to continue sinning does not grant a person the excuse to maintain the same pattern of living. In describing a new creation in Christ, Paul uses the adjectives "kind," "tenderhearted," and "forgiving." These are not natural dispositions of the natural human being; these are supernatural reactions to the broken mess of creation.

SAVED FOR A PURPOSE

Paul says in Romans 5:14 that Christianity is foundationally void and useless if Christ did not resurrect from the dead after his crucifixion. For the Christian, this has massive connotations. If Christ did not rise, he did not conquer death and in turn conquered death on behalf of anyone else. If Christ was not raised, his forgiveness would mean absolutely nothing. Believers cannot understate the grace that must be shown to others in response to the magnificent and unbelievable power exemplified in Jesus Christ. The final words of a risen Savior are not comforting promises of eternity, but an insistence on being light in the midst of darkness (Matt. 28:18-20).

God's will is not aimed entirely at the Christian going to Heaven, but rather for his people to represent him well and live according to his immutable standard in the here and now. The gospel frees us from our own interests. Christians have an obligation to love God and love others well precisely because of the cross.

The character of Christ, this gospel-infused sword we wield, is at the forefront of the Christian witness to a lost world. And Satan cannot deflect its blows. As Jesus proclaims, not even the Gates of Hell can stop his Church (Matt. 16:18).

16

8 CHARACTERISTICS OF SANCTIFICATION
Dustin Crowe

One of the things I enjoyed most about my previous job was the direct connection between how hard I worked and the results I saw. If I just put my head down and pushed hard, I could get where I wanted. It was an independent role and I liked the fact that my production rested on no one's shoulders but my own.

Much of my frustration in growing as a Christian is because sanctification isn't exactly like that job. Yes, my effort does affect my growth, but I can't simply produce the desired outcome from my performance alone. This has not only shaped my own spiritual formation, but it changes how I encourage other believers. When a brother comes to me sharing a struggle with sin, I realize I can't just take him to the mat for not working hard enough—I must take him to the cross to rest in Christ's work for him. I find many Christians genuinely desiring to grow but they end up throwing up their hands in discouragement saying, "I'm trying but things don't seem to be changing." I think as weary believers, we can go from feeling frustrated to feeling free as we take the yoke off our own backs and place it on Jesus.

Gospel-centered sanctification tethers becoming (growing) to being (identity) by making Christ's accomplishments and provision for us the catalyst of our lives. Here are eight characteristics of gospel-centered sanctification that frame our theology of the doctrine while also steering our practice.

1. NEWS, NOT ADVICE

"And this word is the good news that was preached to you" (1 Pt. 1:25).

As Tim Keller points out, the gospel is first and foremost an announcement. It is news about the historical events related to the life, death, and resurrection of the God-man Jesus. And it is good news because the objective events have personal significance; they are for us so we might be redeemed from our sin and reconciled to God. I do my brothers and sisters in Christ little good when I resort to offering sage advice, giving opinions, or dispensing the latest spiritual maxims.

For the gospel (and no shabby replacements) to remain the center, we must regularly remind one another of the good *news* of Jesus Christ. We retell this accomplished, objective, historical news and unpack the never-ending applications gushing from it. If the majority of my conversations sound like "you should try doing this or that" instead of "Jesus has already done this for you" then I'm headed out to the stormy sea of advice and opinion.

2. REPENTANCE, NOT RESOLVE

"Confess your sins to one another" (Jas. 5:16).

The gospel grabs us and shakes us back into the reality we quickly forget: sin is a big deal and our hearts reek of it. I avoid thinking of myself or my sin in these stark terms. I've noticed that instead of confessing my sin, I settle for praying that I would "do better." Instead of seeing my cutting tongue as sin requiring humble repentance I might piously say, "I've not done a good job in my speech this week and I need to make that a higher priority." Through my language of "trying harder" or "being more disciplined" I create the mirage of being a good person. All I need, I tell myself, is to dig deeper into my inner reservoirs of strength and goodness. In reality, I need more

God-dependent and self-humbling repentance and less self-sufficient and God-ignoring resolve.

3. NEEDY, NOT SELF-SUFFICIENT

"God opposes the proud, but he gives grace to the humble" (Jas. 4:6).

Once we turn to repentance from sin instead of improving on our weaknesses, it becomes clear we can't dig out of the problem we got ourselves into. I don't just need more discipline. The problem isn't primarily that I'm not giving it all I've got or trying with enough vigor. The gospel unshackles us by allowing God to be in charge of my sanctification instead of me (deep exhale). When I stop relying on myself and my resources and collapse into trust in God, I see He possesses the power I needed all along.

God promises help to the humble but leaves the self-reliant to their own resources. My generation laughed when Stuart Smalley picked himself up by looking into the mirror and saying, "I'm good enough. I'm strong enough." Unfortunately, we failed to see that this kind of thinking had slipped into how we live our lives.

4. HEART TRANSFORMATION, NOT BEHAVIOR MODIFICATION

"I will put my laws into their minds, and write them on their hearts" (Heb. 8:10).

The biblical view of sanctification requires a genuine change of the heart (root) in order to have the long-term effects of reflecting Christ (fruit). Heart transformation takes time and work. Because most people "don't have time" and don't like work we try to short-circuit this process by simply altering a few behaviors. Since the person hasn't actually changed—including their motives and desires—it's a near-sighted solution at best. For example, instead of actually dealing with the pride in my heart that fuels sarcasm, I just tone it down a couple notches.

If others are less offended by my words then I assume I've fixed the problem. Despite the better version of me on the outside the heart remains unchanged. We might know this cognitively but think how often when someone shares a struggle with sin the first thing they're told is how to work on the behavior. These might be helpful strategies, but they aren't solutions. Care for the root and healthy fruit will eventually ripen.

5. FREEDOM IN CHRIST, NOT SLAVERY TO LAW

"For freedom Christ has set us free; stand firm therefore, and do
    not submit again to a yoke of slavery" (Gal. 5:1).

The gospel promise is that at the moment of faith our condemnation is removed and we are declared righteous—with the results of full acceptance and fatherly love. Hearts changed because of grace are given a stronger motivation than a person striving to merit God's favor through works. Grace jolts us into joy because of an undeserved redemption and we can now live out of gratitude and love for Christ. We seek to grow in sanctification, not to receive favor but as a result of tasting such favor. This does not eliminate the role of law completely, but it does change our relationship to it.

The difference between gospel-centered sanctification and its performance-based counterfeits is that the former prompts heartfelt obedience out of gratitude and the rest provoke external compliance out of guilt. The fruit of the Spirit are not what we bring to God for approval. They are the result of walking in the freedom Christ brings to children freed from the law's enslaving power.

6. UNDER THE RULE OF CHRIST, NOT APART FROM IT

"He has delivered us form the domain of darkness and trans-
    ferred us to the kingdom of his beloved Son" (Col. 1:13).

In the gospel, God heaps good news on top of good news. We're not only freed from slavery to sin and Satan but we're also redeemed to the kingdom of the Son. There we receive the guidance, protection, and presence of the all-powerful King. Imagine if God had freed Israel in Exodus—people who had been slaves all their lives—and then left them in the wilderness. They lacked wisdom, understanding of righteousness, and knowledge of how to live consistently with why they were created. Thankfully, for Israel after the exodus and for Christians after redemption in Christ, God does not leave us as refugees but makes us full-fledged citizens.

When I see sanctification through gospel-centered lenses, living under the rule and reign of Jesus doesn't steal my joy but maximizes it. The biblical concept of kingdom unites gospel and law. God's law for those already in the kingdom is not a criteria for citizenship. Instead, it is just as much a demonstration of his care and grace as it his authority. In Christ's kingdom, his laws are not to be loathed but to be loved, and his rule is not dreadful but delightful.

7. IN COMMUNITY, NOT ISOLATION

> "And let us consider how to stir up one another to love and good works" (Heb. 10:24).

Many of the frustrations and shortcomings in the Christian life occur from trying to play a team-sport on our own. The kid playing basketball alone in his driveway never becomes great without instructional coaching, the complementary strengths of his teammates, and the sharpening of skills that only comes from other people. When we start thinking we're strong enough and good enough on our own we believe self-reliant lies opposed to a gospel of need. If you're not in a biblical community focused on Jesus and anchored in the authority of the Word, who will ask tough questions when you choose sin or share your joys when God is faithful? Who will speak the gospel of grace when you think you've blown it? Who will pray with you when you feel alone or shaken in your faith?

Sanctification within community is a two-way street. God matures us as others love us in word and deed, but he also strengthens us by stretching us to share our faith, serve with our gifts, and enter into messy relationships—which all of them are of course. Being plugged into a church body and committing to grow in maturity alongside others isn't an option. Gospel-centered sanctification only happens as you humbly receive the gospel and the gifts other believers bring to you, and then doggedly commit to doing the same for them in return.

8. PROGRESSION, NOT PERFECTION

"But one thing I do: forgetting what lies behind and straining forward to what lies ahead" (Phil. 3:13).

Unfortunately, we often talk in a way that fosters misunderstandings about what the Christian life will look like. Our speech can make it sound like the Christian's life should be characterized by complete victory over sin instead of continued repentance from sin. Martin Luther provides a good counterbalance in Thesis 1 of his famous 95 Theses: "When our Lord and Master Jesus Christ said 'Repent,' he intended that the entire life of believers should be repentance." In this life, we will always remain simultaneously sinners and saints—people who have been justified and yet remain nagged by indwelling sin.

The Puritans portrayed this lifelong perseverance in their picture of the Christian carrying a weight on his back but the Word in his hand on his pilgrimage to the celestial city. Since we never arrive at perfection in this life we must daily bring our sins before God and receive fresh grace from his hand. We not only confess our sins but we by faith look to Christ to find assurance of our forgiveness and the help to change. This is why many church liturgies include confession of sin and assurance of pardon, modeling the rhythm of our own lives. Just as sure as the sun comes up after the night so also we awake daily in need of grace that pardons and grace to persevere.

17

THE PEOPLE WE'RE BECOMING
Jeremy Carr

I love the movie *A Beautiful Mind*. The acting, story, and music are all superb. The first time I saw the movie, I was caught by surprise by the twist at the end—the revelation of what was *truly* occurring in the life and mind of the main character. With this new insight, *A Beautiful Mind* became one of my favorite movies. Having knowledge of the ending and understanding the truth in no way lessened my enjoyment of the movie, but rather excited me as I was able to watch the movie numerous times, seeing truths that I had previously missed. Similarly, the doctrine of illumination is not only initial, but ongoing—a continuous work of the Holy Spirit giving believers insight and wisdom through Scripture (Jn. 14:25-26).

While initial illumination is involved in regeneration (being brought from death to life in Christ), ongoing illumination is involved in sanctification. Sanctification is the process of being made holy and set apart for holy use. Millard Erickson explains,

> Although regeneration is instantaneously complete, it is not an end in itself. As a change of spiritual impulses, regeneration is the beginning of a process of growth that continues throughout one's lifetime. This process of spiritual maturation is sanctification. Sanctification is the ongoing transformation of character so that the believer's life actually comes to mirror the standing he or she already has in God's sight.

Sanctification is the work of God's Holy Spirit dwelling in us (see: John Murray, *Redemption: Accomplished and Applied*). The Word is the primary means of the work of the Holy Spirit. Sanctification, therefore, is the work of the Spirit with the Word. Sanctification is a work of the Holy Spirit that has both happened and continues to happen. As a completed event, Scripture teaches definitive sanctification in that believers have been "sanctified through the Holy Spirit" (Rom. 15:16), "were washed" and "were sanctified" (1 Cor. 6:11), and "were sealed for the day of redemption" (Eph. 4:30). Likewise, sanctification is a continual process as believers live in holiness (1 Thess. 4:7-8) as the word of God "is at work in you" (2 Thess. 2:13), for obedience to Jesus Christ (1 Pt. 1:2). Sanctification is both an event and a process of the Holy Spirit whose principle means is Scripture.

According to Charles Hodge, the Holy Spirit enlightens the mind of the believer enabling him to see "all the great doctrines of the Bible concerning God, Christ, and things spiritual and eternal . . . revealed by this inward teaching of the Spirit." The Holy Spirit operates through the Scriptures, "For the word of God is living and active, sharper than any two-edged sword, piercing to the division of soul and of spirit, of joints and of marrow, and discerning the thoughts and intentions of the heart" (Heb. 4:12). This active work through the Word grows our understanding of Scripture through interpretation and obedience, both personally and corporately.

INTERPRETATION

"Longview made dookie go gold." This statement may sound nonsensical, ridiculous, or even profane out of context. However, this is a quote from the punk rock documentary "One Nine Nine Four" referring to the album "Dookie" by Green Day, whose single "Longview" launched the band to international fame and gave the album gold status. Context is important, not only for this musical quote, but more so for our understanding and application of Scripture. Apart from the Holy Spirit working in our hearts and minds, Scripture will not make sense and achieve within us the Author's intent.

The work of the Holy Spirit through Scripture in illumination, both in initial regeneration and ongoing sanctification, has both personal and community implications. How believers understand these implications involves interpretation. The text has one meaning that the interpreter must understand and apply. That meaning is whatever the author intended the meaning to be (Walter Kaiser, *Toward an Exegetical Theology*). Theology cannot be separated from the text.

Illumination involves the work of the Holy Spirit "assisting the reader to achieve clarity in understanding the content of the Word." (R.C. Sproul, *The Internal Testimony of the Holy Spirit*). This assistance happens personally to the individual as well as to the community. This conviction is not against reason, but beyond reason.

The Holy Spirit illumines the mind and inwardly teaches so that the Word renders faith "superior to all opinion." Jesus promised that the Holy Spirit will "guide you into all the truth" (Jn. 16:13). We therefore act in obedience with faith; we are to trust and obey. While we have "faith seeking understanding," our understanding is not a prerequisite for obedience. Often in and through obedience we grow in greater understanding as the Holy Spirit's work of illumination brings forth our sanctification and empowered obedience.

The Holy Spirit's inward work happens to individual hearts and minds. Working simultaneously through the Word and in the heart and mind of the hearer, the Spirit does not operate independently from the Word in illumination. To dismiss personal illumination is to neglect the Holy Spirit's work through the Word.

BOTH THE MEANS AND THE RESULT

Sanctification is characterized by ongoing understanding of and application of the Scriptures. Paul writes, "Now we have received not the spirit of the world, but the Spirit who is from God, that we might understand the things freely given us by God" (1 Cor. 2:12). John writes, "But you have been anointed by the Holy One, and you all have knowledge" (1 Jn. 2:20). Jesus states, "When the Spirit of truth comes, he will guide you into all the truth, for he will not speak on his own authority, but whatever he hears he will speak, and he will declare to you the things that are to come. He will glorify me, for he will take what is mine and declare it to you" (Jn. 16:13-14). We see, therefore, that regeneration is the motivation for obedience. Indeed regeneration is necessary for fruitful application of Scripture.

Scripture is the root for both faith and practice. When God speaks, man is required to obey. Authority implies obedience. The authority of Christ and Scripture is both bestowed and inherent, therefore we submit to God's authority. We are to obey even if we do not understand because the authority of Scripture rests not in our minds or perceptions, but in God's Word. Scripture is God's authoritative and revelatory Word, inspired by the Holy Spirit who also illumines the believer so that the truth of God can be applied.

Application of Scripture is for both personal and corporate sanctification. Colossians 3:16 instructs, "Let the word of Christ dwell in you richly, teaching and admonishing one another in all wisdom, singing psalms and hymns and spiritual songs, with thankfulness in your hearts to God." Likewise Paul writes in Ephesians 5:19, "addressing one another in psalms and hymns and spiritual songs, singing and making melody to the Lord with your heart." Growing in holiness is both a personal and community occurrence.

EMPOWERED OBEDIENCE

Paul writes in Titus 2:14 how Jesus Christ "gave himself for us to redeem us from all lawlessness and to purify for himself a people for his own possession who are zealous for good works." As people for Christ's own possession, redeemed and purified, we are increasingly given opportunities for good works. As disciples, we experience personal redemption in the context of community on mission. In this we grow as disciples as well as forward the gospel in making disciples.

Obedience gives evidence to both personal and corporate sanctification. Paul writes in Philippians 2:12-13, "Therefore, my beloved, as you have always obeyed, so now, not only as in my presence but much more in my absence, work out your own salvation with fear and trembling, for it is God who works in you, both to will and to work for his good pleasure." This admonition follows the promise, "that he who began a good work in you will bring it to completion at the day of Jesus Christ" (Phil. 1:6). This is understood in the context of the Philippian believers' "partnership" as "saints" in gospel mission.

Illumination, both in regeneration and sanctification, shows us that it is the believer and the community of believers who are changed, not Scripture. The Christian life, therefore, is not only *doing* transformative things, but *being* a transformed people. Paul writes to Titus,

> For the grace of God has appeared, bringing salvation
> for all people, training us to renounce ungodliness and
> worldly passions, and to live self-controlled, upright,
> and godly lives in the present age, waiting for our
> blessed hope, the appearing of the glory of our great
> God and Savior Jesus Christ, who gave himself for us to
> redeem us from all lawlessness and to purify for him-
> self a people for his own possession who are zealous
> for good works. (Titus 2:11-14)

Transformed identity, both personally and corporately, results in obedience. Murray writes that Scripture confirms "this great truth that regeneration is such a radical, pervasive, and efficacious transformation that it immediately registers itself in the conscious activity of the person concerned in the exercises of faith and repentance and new obedience."

The application of Scripture to the believer's life is the work of the Holy Spirit. Like sanctification, this is an ongoing process. This ongoing application of the Word by the Holy Spirit affects the intellect as well as the will. The result is obedient action rooted in faith. Scott Hafemann connects faith and obedience with God's Word: "Faith is trusting God to do what he has promised because we are convinced by his provisions that God is willing and able to keep his word."

As Scripture reveals the nature and character of God our rightful response is to obey. Hafemann continues,

Faith in God is an active dependence on his word that always expresses itself in action. The reason for this unity of faith and obedience as two aspects of our one response to God is the promises of God are always organically linked to corresponding commands. Every command of God is built on a promise from God. Therefore every divine call to action (obedience) is, at the same time, a divine summons to trust in God's promises (faith) . . . trust in God's promise would mean obedience to his commands.

The Holy Spirit works in and through Scripture to actualize our faith and empower obedience, therefore we must depend on the Holy Spirit. Scripture testifies to both initial and ongoing illumination, both of which are closely tied to the Word. Faith and obedience depend on the continued work of the Holy Spirit with and through Scripture.

MISSION

The mission to "make disciples" is an act of empowered obedience. Jesus states in Acts 1:8, "But you will receive power when the Holy Spirit has come upon you, and you will be my witnesses in Jerusalem and in all Judea and Samaria, and to the end of the earth." The disciples, empowered by the Holy Spirit, were on mission locally, regionally, and globally to "make disciples of all nations . . . teaching them to observe all that I have commanded you" (Matt. 28:19-20). The mission is under the authority of Christ, empowered by the Spirit, and saturated with Scripture. This is consistent with God's instruction in Deuteronomy 6:4-9 (which Jesus quotes as the greatest commandment):

Hear, O Israel: The Lord our God, the Lord is one. You shall love the Lord your God with all your heart and with all your soul and with all your might. And these words that I command you today shall be on your heart. You shall teach them diligently to your children,

and shall talk of them when you sit in your house, and
when you walk by the way, and when you lie down,
and when you rise. You shall bind them as a sign on
your hand, and they shall be as frontlets between your
eyes. You shall write them on the doorposts of your
house and on your gates.

In this passage, Israel is instructed in missional discipleship. Reminded of their identity as God's people and his authority as their God, they are instructed to "teach" what God has
"commanded." They do so in all areas of life: personally ("you"),
family ("children"), community ("house"), and culture ("gates").
This missional rhythm is as they go about life: "when you sit,"
"when you walk," "when you lie down," "when you rise." Likewise, a missional rhythm is included in the great commission.
The imperative to "make disciples" is by "going, teaching, and
baptizing." As this mission continues for us today, D.A. Carson
writes, "The Kingdom of God advances by the power of the
Spirit through the ministry of the Word."

SANCTIFYING DISCIPLESHIP

We must ask ourselves: Are we growing in holiness personally?
Are we growing in holiness in community? As we increase in
information and application, are we growing in transformation?

Sanctification is not just *knowing* about holiness and *doing*
holy things. Sanctification is about *being* and *becoming* holy
people. Illumination is both the means and result of transformation and missional obedience gives evidence to this transformation. We return to 2 Timothy 3:16-17, "All Scripture is
breathed out by God and profitable for teaching, for rebuke, for
correction, and for training in righteousness, that the man of
God may be competent, equipped for every good work." We
must not overlook the truth that this equipping is a work of the
Holy Spirit who, through "the sacred writings . . . make[s] you
wise for salvation through faith in Christ Jesus" (2 Tim. 3:15)
which then identifies one as a "man of God." We see that this is
not about making oneself good, but about being redeemed. Re-

demption is an identity change, not just behavior modification. 2 Timothy 3:16 is about righteous faith and character that manifests in obedience.

Since the Holy Spirit works through and with the Bible, we have a permanent need for his work.

We do so with confidence in Scripture as the written promises of God.

Scripture is a generous gift from the generous Father revealing the generous Son by the generous Holy Spirit to people transformed to be his generous church: saints in partnership in the gospel. The new community of disciples relates in the gospel and grows in understanding and interpretation of Scripture. Likewise, we grow together in obedience and application of Scripture as a community on mission with the gospel.

18

4 ANCHORS OF REPENTANCE
Jake Ledet

Repentance is a big deal. You've probably heard that. It's a motif in Scripture that you absolutely cannot avoid. We often create terminology, systems, or routines that help to motivate and remind us to regularly repent because we see its importance. This surely isn't bad. However, complicated theological definitions and white-knuckled systems often lead to a dry, mechanical, lifeless interaction with God. This, of course, is bad.

The most common definition of repentance that I have heard is to turn *from* your sin and turn *to* Jesus. This is a helpful definition, but if we let a definition drive our repentance, it isn't really repentance.

So, what drives repentance? What type of repentance is truly biblical? The scope of this question is deep and wide, but I think there are four foundational aspects of biblical repentance: biblical repentance is from God, centered on God, produces life-giving joy, and should be sought in community.

1. BIBLICAL REPENTANCE IS FROM GOD
If we look at Psalm 130, we see the Psalmist waiting, seeking, and needing God. It seems as if, without God, there is no hope. Biblical repentance starts with God. The Psalmist later cries out in the midst of repentance saying, "Cast me not away from your presence, and take not your Holy Spirit from me" (Ps. 51:11). David knows that there is no hope for repentance outside of the Holy Spirit's leading. He is petitioning God to grant him forgiveness. We also witness Paul encourage Timothy to correct

his opponents with gentleness, so that "God may perhaps grant them repentance" (2 Tim. 2:25).

Biblical repentance is initiated by God. How is this helpful? If God grants repentance, then we have no need to fake it. That doesn't mean we give ourselves over to sin while we wait for God to grant repentance. Surely if your heart heads in that direction, there is cause for concern. But, the truth that God grants repentance should drive us to seek him earnestly. Instead of settling for going through some routine, we ask the God of the universe to brake our hearts over our sin. Scripture also encourages us to "draw near to the throne of grace with confidence" (Heb. 4:16). God is willing and able not only to respond, but to give generously.

Why does appealing to God often feel difficult? Perhaps it's because we want God to zap us from a distance rather than seek him in the midst of disobedience. Our mechanical, humdrum repentance is dry because we don't want to be intimate with God. We have blown it, perhaps for the thousandth time, and facing the most offended Person is unbelievably humbling. But in this, we have forgotten another aspect of biblical repentance. We are told that not only should we approach God with confidence, but that "God's kindness is meant to lead you to repentance" (Rom 2:4).

We don't seek God for repentance because we are good, but because he is good. David's opening cry in Psalm 51 rings with desperation, "Have mercy on me, O God, according to your steadfast love; according to your abundant mercy blot out my transgression." David bases his plea on God's mercy.

Jesus's words remind us ever-so-clearly that we need God's mercy. Consider the Jesus's parable to those who trusted in themselves that they were righteous while treating others with contempt:

> "Two men went up into the temple to pray, one a
> Pharisee and the other a tax collector. The Pharisee,
> standing by himself, prayed thus: 'God, I thank you
> that I am not like other men, extortioners, unjust, adul-
> terers, or even like this tax collector. I fast twice a

week; I give tithes of all that I get.' But the tax collector,
standing far off, would not even lift up his eyes to
heaven, but beat his breast, saying, 'God, be merciful to
me, a sinner!' I tell you, this man went down to his
house justified, rather than the other. For everyone
who exalts himself will be humbled, but the one who
humbles himself will be exalted." (Lk. 18:9-14)

We tend resemble the tax collector at times when things go
badly. But does the rhythm of our lives consistently communicate the same need for mercy? Do you more often resemble the
Pharisee, bartering with God based on your own deeds? You go
to church, tithe, read Christian blogs, and even share the gospel
at times. Those these things are right and good, they do not necessarily mirror a heart seeking after the God who grants forgiveness.

Entitlement to grace creeps into our life subtly. It's an
insidious disease. One way entitlement manifests in our lives is
blaming God for our sin. Have you ever said, "God I do all of
this stuff for you, why have you not saved me from _____ sin."
Maybe we don't say it in those words, but we know that God has
the power to help overcome any sin, and yet he hasn't. Entitlement rears its ugly head.

We must remember that our repentance will be maturing
until we go on to glory. Holy Spirit led, God-centered, life-giving,
joyful repentance is a gift you continue to discover for the rest
of your life. And the good news is that God wants to give it to
you.

2. BIBLICAL REPENTANCE IS GOD-CENTERED

In Psalm 51, David also laments, "Against you, you only, have I
sinned and done what is evil in your sight, so that you may be
justified in your words and blameless in your judgment" (Ps.
51:4).

At times, our repentance can be centered on everything but
God. If we were to think of repentance as a play, then God is the
main character while sin, ourselves, and others play supporting
roles. However, we are often grieved over our sin because we

are tired of being the guy that struggles with porn or the mom that blows up at her kids. Sometimes we don't like when relationships are off or that our workplace or church has issues. Our response is to try and make everything right again, but this will get us nowhere.

In these situations, we should join in with David, recalling that our sin can only be called sin because God himself declares what is holy and what is not. People are affected, no doubt, but God is always the most offended. In repentance, we have the obligation to going before the most offended party and acknowledging our guilt without excuse. If repentance isn't God-centered, we can give him a token apology while avoiding facing the depth of our sin. Unfortunately, this causes us to miss enjoying the most abundant, heavenly pardon ever offered: our sin for the Son's perfect righteousness. Jesus righteousness feels most undeserved when we are aware of our sin, and our heart rejoices most deeply when God is at the center of our repentance. Our joy in repentance is intimately intertwined with God's work to crush sin for the glory of his name. He reminds us in Isaiah:

> "For my name's sake I defer my anger, for the sake of my praise I restrain it for you, that I may not cut you off. Behold, I have refined you, but not as silver; I have tried you in the furnace of affliction. For my own sake, for my own sake, I do it, for how should my name be profaned? My glory I will not give to another." (Is. 48:9-11)

3. BIBLICAL REPENTANCE LEADS TO LIFE-GIVING JOY

Repentance should lead to joy, as Scripture often reminds us. For example:

> "For godly grief produces a repentance that leads to salvation without regret, whereas worldly grief produces death." (2 Cor. 7:10)

"Let me hear joy and gladness; let the bones that you have broken rejoice." (Ps. 51:8)

"Restore to me the joy of your salvation, and uphold me with a willing spirit." (Ps. 51:12)

Taking our sin seriously and experiencing the joy of repentance can and should come in many forms. Surely we have had times where our brokenness over sin has led to genuine godly grief and tears have flowed. But there are often times genuine repentance takes place in the midst of ordinary life. Here is a brief personal vignette:

I have some friends that raise chickens. One night, they were telling us about the death of a chicken and my buddy mentioned that chickens will often pluck the eyes out of their dead counterparts. He even said as a joke that if you lied down out there, they would pluck your eyes out. My young son, Wyatt, loves the chickens.

I was at work remembering the conversation with my friend and realizing my son was over at their house. I had the ridiculous picture of my son lying down near the chickens and getting his eyes plucked out. I realize this sounds quite silly, but it caused real anxiety in me. I called my wife and couldn't get in touch with her. I was going to have her check on Wyatt's eyes. Then the Lord brought to mind a struggle of mine.

I have realized more and more that I struggle to trust God with my kids. I often feel the need to over-control situations because, frankly, I don't trust God. I happen to be dwelling on Psalm 130 that week, and I remembered the Psalmist exhortation at the end: "O Israel, hope in the Lord!" I then began tell myself, "Jake, hope in the Lord!" A sweet joy came over my heart as I ventured from lies to truth, sinful disobedience to Spirit-led obedience.

This is a picture of repentance in the everyday rhythm of life. If we are to be more consistent and genuine in our repentance, we must realize God grants this gift in many different forms, although the substance is the same. Whether at church, at home, at work, or anywhere else, joy can be had if we simply focus on the One who offers it to us.

4. BIBLICAL REPENTANCE IS SOUGHT IN COMMUNITY

It's important to note that these three aspects of repentance should not be sought alone. There is great joy in seeing a sister who has been asking God to mold her into the image of his Son come to the place of repentance. Joy abounds. It's beautiful to be a part of a community where people don't just talk about some abstract theology of repentance, but who actually point each other to the God who grants repentance. As with most things, it is hard to be a pointer if you aren't a practitioner. But as you swim in the abundant grace available for you in repentance, your spirit will be renewed.

As we walk through the highs and lows of life with others, we shouldn't feel a heavy burden to "fix" them our make sure they "get it." We continually walk humbly with them, trusting them to the only One who is able to save. The Psalms are very helpful in this regard. We see men experiencing and interacting with God. We don't merely want people to see their sin; we want them to see their sin in relationship to a holy, forgiving God.

Repentance is not simply an individual affair. Repentance experienced in community allows us to share in each other's joy and marvel at God's good grace. So take heart, and seek him for the gift of repentance. May the Spirit blow a fresh wind into your soul. And may you have the courage to share it with others.

19

5 LIES THAT KILL OBEDIENCE
Brad Watson

When Mirela and I loaded up our belongings and headed to the Northwest, we were filled with an incredible blend of expectation and zeal. We knew something major was happening, and God was going to let us be part of it. We didn't have a grand plan. We just had a genuine desire to serve and to start a church in Portland. It was a big adventure and we felt like pioneers on the Oregon Trail. As we crossed the Walla Walla Mountains in eastern Oregon, we listened to Rich Mullen's song, "You're on the Verge of a Miracle." We couldn't wait to see mass revival in Portland.

God placed us in a remarkable church planting team. We've seen lots of evidence of God's grace in our lives and in the church. He has continually provided for our small church plant. We are thankful for many things. From the outside, it looks pretty good. Church planters come from all over the world to learn about what we are doing. Our missional communities multiply every year. We even have a cool website.

The reality is: life lived on the frontier is hard. We have seen only a handful of people come to Christ and be baptized. Church conflict is constant. It seems as though every time someone joins our church, another person leaves. About a third of the missional communities we start fail. All the while, our city continues to be desperately far from knowing the riches of the gospel. My neighbors constantly reject the good news of Jesus despite our best attempts to demonstrate and proclaim it to them. The city is not flourishing in the peace of salvation, but struggling in the chaos of brokenness. It doesn't feel like the 'miracle' is happening. We sometimes wonder if revival will come and if we'll be around to see it.

LESSONS FROM CHINA

It reminds me of the church in China. No, not the Chinese church of today, where thousands are baptized daily and they can't print enough Bibles or equip enough pastors to keep up with the rapid multiplication of the church. Not that movement. I am reminded of the Chinese churches of Hudson Taylor, Robert Morrison, and the Cambridge Seven. They spent the best years of their lives laboring with little or no fruit. Despite decades of evangelism and service, they only witnessed a few conversions and a few new churches in their lifetimes. By the time Mao banned religion, many, even within the missions movement, assumed China was unreachable. These missionaries had seemingly wasted their lives.

However, the house church movement that began to erupt in the 1960s and continues today was built on the foundation of these missionaries. The converts they baptized became the backbone of today's movement. The few disciples they made, made more disciples, and they made disciples, and so on. The revival those missionaries prayed for came. It was just decades after they had died. The pioneering missionaries never saw the packed house churches or the all night baptism services. They didn't see their prayers answered. Yet, they faithfully served, at great personal cost, for years. They obeyed the call to go and make disciples without knowing their impact.

THE REWARDS OF OBEDIENCE

What do you get for all your anonymous and resultless faithfulness? Nothing short of God himself. "Discipleship," as Bonhoefer writes, "means joy." The reward is Christ himself. Often we get confused and think the rewards for obedience are big churches, lots of twitter followers, and the approval of our peers. We miss the promise of Christ.

How sick are we when we lust for the results of Christ's work, thinking it could belong to us? When we prefer conversion stories to Christ? Sadly, many of us will hope more for "success" than we will hope for Christ.

If you follow Jesus, you may never see revival. Though you love your city, you may never see it transformed. But if you follow Jesus you are guaranteed this one thing: Jesus. Your fruit *is* the joy of obeying Jesus. Nothing else. The baptisms and church plants belong to God. Those are God's work, not yours.

5 LIES THAT KILL OBEDIENCE
Our ability to quit and become sidetracked is great. Our hearts are constantly being attacked by lies that keep us from persevering in faith. These five lies are particularly successful. They are deceptive and effective in killing our conviction to follow Jesus and trust in his work.

1. "You are above this."
This is the lie of strong pride. That the grunt work isn't for you. I first heard this lie when I cleaned toilets for a church in Los Angeles. You may hear it while you are watching babies in the nursery Sunday after Sunday. Or when you get stood up once again by your not-yet believing friends for dinner. You hear it when your neighbors shun you for being crazy people who believe in Jesus. The lie is: "You are better than this." When you believe this lie, you think you are entitled to fame. In reality, you are only entitled to be called a child of God, and that right was purchased by Christ. Don't settle for position and fame. If you think you are above the job and task, you will not persevere in obedience.

2. "You are below this."
Many times it also sounds like: "You don't belong and you don't deserve this." This is a lie attacking Christ's ability to work in and through you. If you believe this lie, you believe that God is not at work, but that you are the one at work. This lie leads to fear and rejection of your identity as a son or daughter of God. It is also born out of comparison to others instead of the supremacy of Christ. What's devastating about this lie is that it paralyzes folks from the obedience that would give God glory.

No one is capable or skilled enough to do what God has called them to do. But the Holy Spirit empowers us for the tasks and God is glorified in using us.

3. "If you were better, it would be easier."

This one comes when things feel incredibly hard. It leads to self-loathing and increased suffering. This lie shakes your sense of purpose. You begin to place yourself as the focal point of God's work and conclude you are either in the way or driving it forward. When things improve, you believe it is because you have done better and have earned it. When things fail, you are certain it is your fault. Similar lies are: "You have to be good to be used for good." Or: "You have to be smarter, better, quicker, more talented, more educated, rich and moral in order to do good." This leads to a personal quest for self-rightness, excellence, and God's job. This lie essentially says: "You are this city's savior." Eventually you quit in desperation because you have labored without *the* Savior.

4. "If it isn't happening now, it never will."

This lie says: "Today is all there is and God can't work tomorrow. If God hasn't answer your prayers for revival by now, he never will." When you believe it, you lose perspective on the scope of life and count everything you are doing as worthless. You are no longer content in obedience alone, but want to see what your obedience will create. This is nearsighted dreaming. This lie results in quick quitting or shrinking versions of worthwhile-God-given dreams. This is a lie people believe when the settle for less than the radical surrender and obedience God called them to. When we believe this lie we are saying, "God doesn't care anymore or he can't do it."

5. "You are alone."

This is the hardest one. Our sinful hearts leap to this lie when we are tired and discouraged. The goal of this lie is to isolate you and make you think no one else cares, and no one else is coming to help. No longer are you being obedient to God's work, but now you feel like a hired hand. It is as if God is paying you to establish a franchise of his kingdom and is looking for a return on his investment. Your belief in this lie says, "Jesus doesn't love me or this city. He didn't died for this city or for me—God abandons his people."

GOSPEL MOTIVATION

At the heart of each these lies is an attack on your motivation and an attack on the gospel. The truth is Christ died for you. You are loved and you are his son or daughter (1 Jn. 3:1). He has empowered you with his Spirit to be his witness (Acts 1:8). He will work in you and through you as he works all things together for good and conforms you to the likeness of Christ (Rom. 8:28-29). He is with you always, even to the end of the age (Matt. 28).

When I was 11, my family moved to Lisbon, a city of five million people with fewer than 4 percent believing the gospel. Shortly after we arrived, my family went to a hill that overlooked the city we came to "win" for Christ. My dad wept over it as he prayed for the people and for the gospel to take root in their hearts. We all cried. We had put everything on the line to follow Jesus to this city. We loved the city and we loved Jesus.

It's been nearly two decades since that day we prayed for the city, and the statistics are the same. My parents saw only a couple of people baptized in over a decade of ministry there. They will never see or experience his prayers for the city being answered.

Are you willing to weep over your city for decades and never see your prayers answered, to plant seeds you may never see germinate? What if your church never becomes nationally known? What if you don't write books or speak at conferences? Is the gift of the gospel enough for you?

20

8 KEYS TO PERSONAL PRAYER
Winfield Bevins

*We look upon prayer as a means of getting things for ourselves;
the Bible's idea of prayer is that we may get to know God himself.*
—Oswald Chambers

Prayer is first and foremost a personal relationship with Jesus Christ. Some people think of prayer like a business transaction or as something they have to do just like checking something off a to-do list. But that isn't really prayer at all. Think of prayer in intimate terms, like a conversation between close friends. What are some words that you think of when you think of an intimate friendship? You will probably think of words like loving, caring, warm, sincere, personal, and intimate. These are words that should be used to describe our prayer time with the Lord. Prayer should not be dry or stuffy; it should be warm and intimate.

How can you develop a personal prayer life?

BEFORE YOU PRAY
Before praying, there are four things that we should take into consideration. First, schedule a regular prayer time. Find a time every day to spend in prayer. The important thing is that we should be consistent. The psalmist said that he prayed seven times a day. Second, choose a private place to pray. A prayer closet could be anywhere as long as it is private. You can use your garage, pantry, front porch, or any other creative place where you can get alone with God. Some people pray while

driving in their car and others pray while working-out or running. Third, try to limit distractions. Don't pray in the same room that you may watch television or be tempted by other activities. Lastly, have a prayer list to guide your prayers that includes family, friends, church, etc. This will ensure that you don't forget important things to pray for.

KEYS TO PERSONAL PRAYER

Every believer can have a dynamic personal prayer life. The Bible gives us the keys that we need to develop a powerful prayer life. The Scriptures are full of examples of men and women who walked with God and used prayer to impact their world and you can do the same thing through prayer. The following are Scriptural ways you can develop a deeper more fulfilling personal prayer life.

1. Pray In Jesus's Name

Real prayer is Christological, focusing on the person and work of Jesus Christ. There are numerous New Testament references that talk about the importance of praying in the name of Jesus. Jesus himself said, "Most assuredly, I say to you, whatever you ask the Father in my name he will give you" (Jn. 16:23). When we pray in the name of Jesus, God the Father hears us. He responds to the prayer that is offered in the name of his Son Jesus because our relationship with God is through the Son.

2. Pray According to God's Will

God is not a Santa Claus in the sky; he does not give us anything we ask for. But in 1 John 5:14 it says, "If we ask anything according to his will, he hears us." This means that when we pray in accordance with his will we can expect an answer. This is why the Lord's Prayer says, "Thy will be done on earth as it is in Heaven."

3. Scriptural Prayer

One the best ways to pray is to pray according to the Scriptures. John 15:7 says, "If you abide in me, and my word abides in you, you will ask what you desire, and it shall be done for you." If

God's word is in us then his desires become our desires and we can have the assurance that he will answer our prayers. Make sure that your prayers are in line with Scripture. The Lord always honors his Word. A great example is the Lord's Prayer.

4. Keep Commandments
God honors those who honor his Commandments. Jesus said, "Whatever we ask we receive from him, because we keep his commandments and do those things that are pleasing in his sight" (1 Jn. 3:22). If you keep his Commandments and do what is pleasing, then you can be assured that he will hear your prayers.

5. Believe
The Lord wants us to have faith that he will hear our prayers. Jesus said, "And whatever things you ask in prayer, believing, you will receive" (Matt. 21:22). In the great faith chapter of the Bible, we are told that, "without faith it is impossible to please him, for he who comes to God must believe that he is, and that He is the rewarder of those who diligently seek him" (Heb. 11:6). The Lord promises to respond to our prayer of faith.

6. Pray in the Spirit
The Holy Spirit is the Spirit of prayer. Paul tells us to pray at all times in the Spirit. Romans 8:26 reads, "Likewise the Spirit also helps us in our weaknesses. For we do not know what we should pray for as we ought, but the Spirit himself makes intercession for us with groanings which cannot be uttered." We don't always know how to pray and we don't always feel like praying. Therefore we need the Spirit's power to help us pray.

7. Be Persistent
Don't give up if you haven't received an answer to your prayers. Throughout the Bible there are stories of men and women who persevered in prayer. In Luke 18:1-8 there was a little old widow who did not lose heart. James tells us that the effectual fervent prayer of a righteous man avails much.

8. Humble Yourself

Lastly, we are to humble ourselves in prayer. James 4:10 tells us to humble ourselves before the Lord, and he will exalt us. One of my favorite parables about prayer is in Luke 18:9-14, where the Pharisee and tax collector come before God. The Pharisee was proud and boastful, while the tax collector was humble and asked for God's mercy. We are told that God hears the prayer of the humble. If we humble ourselves in the sight of God he will lift us up.

CLOSING PRAYER

Lord, teach us to pray. We ask that you would make us humble, help us be persistent, and give your Holy Spirit to help us pray. We ask that you would cleanse our hearts, meet our needs, heal our hurts, and give us strength to call on your name and to give you glory. In the name of your Son Jesus we pray. Amen.

21

REDEEMING WORSHIP
Matt Oakes

> *Look carefully then how you walk, not as unwise but as wise,*
> *making the best use of the time, because the days are evil. There-*
> *fore do not be foolish, but understand what the will of the Lord is.*
> *And do not get drunk with wine, for that is debauchery, but be*
> *filled with the Spirit, addressing one another in psalms and*
> *hymns and spiritual songs, singing and making melody to the*
> *Lord with your heart, giving thanks always and for everything to*
> *God the Father in the name of our Lord Jesus Christ, submitting*
> *to one another out of reverence for Christ.*
> —Ephesians 5:15-21

When we gather as a church, we demonstrate our worship of God in a number of ways. Some of us worship through setting up for our gathering. Some of us worship by teaching in a children's ministry. Some worship through playing music. Some worship through greeting visitors. The list could go on.

In our missional communities, some of us worship by leading the discussion. Some worship by preparing food for the group. Some worship by coordinating our group's service projects in the community. These are all great ways to demonstrate worship through gratefulness to God by serving one another. Again, the list could go on.

In Ephesians 5, Paul specifically addresses our singing as a church. He gives us three ways that we are to live out our worship through gratefulness and service to one another.

First, we address one another with songs, hymns, and spiritual songs. Second, we give thanks to God. Third, we serve one another. Another way we could look at these is: worship of God that results from the gospel is expressed horizontally (to one another) and vertically (to God) as a redemption of our time together.

VERTICAL

Singing is a gift God has given us to better know him and experience him. In Colossians 3:16, Paul tells the church to *"let the word of Christ dwell in you richly, teaching and admonishing one another is psalms, hymns and spiritual songs."* How does singing allow the Word of God to dwell in us richly? It allows us to express the truth of the gospel and our grateful response to the gospel in ways that are more emotive and meaningful than if we just said them. For example, we often sing hymns or spiritual songs. The song can be incredibly emotional. It is often a sort of battle cry of commitment to God for us to sing as a church. When I just recite the words to most hymns, it's not very inspiring. It sounds like I'm planning a carpool. The melody of the songs connect to what we are called to: following God on his mission, remembering what Christ has done, worshiping God. Songs allows us to express all these things in a way that is much more heartfelt.

The music also helps us remember God's goodness and truth. Chances are, you can recite the first verse of "Amazing Grace," but if I asked you to recite the first four sentences of this article back to me, you couldn't (even though this article is *so much* like poetry). Singing is a great way to learn the truth about God. What we sing gets stuck in our heads. What we sing works its way into our hearts.

Like everything in life, music can either draw us into deeper fellowship with God or draw us away from him and toward our desires. That's why as worship leader, I strive so hard to only sing songs that accurately represent the truth and beauty of God. God has given us music to help us internalize and embody his truth. What we sing forms us as followers of God. In the early church, there was a heretic named Arius who taught that Christ had not existed eternally but had been created by God, and so was not equal to God. And one of the ways he attempted to spread this very false doctrine was by writing catchy songs that contained his heretical theology. This worked for a time, until Ambrose of Milan countered by writing equally catchy songs that reflected the truth of God.

Music helps us remember and hold to the truth of God because our songs about God combine both the intellectual truth about God and our emotional response to those truths. Singing about God gets his truth stuck in our hearts, and as it dwells there richly, it draws us into deeper communion with him.

But many of us have a hard time with singing. We see the command to "make melody to the Lord with our hearts," and it seems weird. "Making melody" is not an everyday occurrence for most of us. When your boss asks you why you took an extra fifteen minutes on your lunch break, you never say, "Well I got caught up making melody in my heart." You'd get some strange looks. Some of us are timid to sing with the church because we feel like our voices aren't good enough. Maybe someone told us we weren't good singers and now whenever we attempt to sing, all we can hear is that person's voice in the back of our head telling us how bad we sound. But the gospel frees us from all of these hang-ups.

Men, let me briefly speak to you. Jesus wept for you, he was in anguish for you so deep that he sweat blood. If Jesus is the ultimate man, there is no shame in showing sorrow for your sin. Jesus has already cried harder than you ever will over your sin. But sorrow wasn't the only emotion Jesus showed. He showed anger over injustice and the manipulation of the poor when he trashed the tables of the priestly charlatans in the temple. He showed joy as he raised his friend Lazarus from the dead. Men, the gospel compels us to express these same emotions. We should rage at our sin. We should weep at the brokenness of our world. We should rejoice in the conquering of our sin by Christ's life, death, and resurrection. And our singing is a great place to begin to express these Christ-like emotions. Our singing is a great place to express the worship of God.

For those of us who do not feel that we sing well enough, and so we sing quietly (if at all). The gospel frees us from our fear, as well. We sing because God has shown us favor in spite of our abilities. We don't sing to earn God's favor. Your ability to be pitch perfect cannot save you! Your voice cannot get up on a cross and die for you, and it cannot get out of the grave and conquer death for you. That has already been accomplished by Christ, and that is why you are called to sing. So don't think that your voice needs to be good enough in order for you to sing with the church. None of our voices are good enough for God. Christ has been good enough for you, so sing out of joy for what he has done and who he is. We sing because we have been loved and served so perfectly in Christ. Singing is not about us.

One last thought on why some of us may struggle with singing. I live in Austin, "the Live Music Capitol of the World," where it seems like everyone is a musician. Everyone has an opinion. We are used to having whatever kind of music we prefer available to us. Austin locals sometimes pick what church they join based on the music. Some choose not to sing certain songs with the church because we don't like that particular song. I've been guilty of this. And I don't think this practice is unique to Austin.

When we decide what church family to join based on our music preference, we place ourselves at the center of the gathering instead of God. We substitute our preferences as our motive for singing in place of worship of God. We are not the center of our singing. There is only one time a year when you are the center of the song, and that's on your birthday. The gospel frees us from this self-serving mode of singing. Instead of trying to serve our musical needs and tastes, we sing because we have been loved and served so perfectly in Christ. Singing is not about us.

HORIZONTAL

While singing is not about us and our individual tastes, it is about one another. In Ephesians 5 we are told to *address* one another with psalms, hymns, and spiritual songs. Again addressing one another with songs in person is not something we often do. When you meet a friend for coffee, you don't greet them by singing, "Hey, we are getting coffee, and that is neat." Yet the gospel inspires us to encourage one another in song. Do you ever think of singing on Sunday that way? Do you ever think to yourself, "I'm going to sing this song not just because I need to hear it, but because other people need to hear it"?

Sadly many in the church don't view our time together singing as a chance to serve one another. Often we view it as an "intimate" time between "me and Jesus." We have the lights down low, our eyes closed, and the music so loud we can't hear our voices. We simply don't consider one another when we gather. And if we aren't considering one another, if we aren't listening to one another when we sing together, what's the point? Why not just put my headphones on and go sing in my closet? Parking would be easier for everyone else.

To display the fullness of the gospel in worship, we need each other. We need the testimony and the encouragement of hearing one another sing the truth about God. We need to be formed by the Word of God dwelling richly in all of our hearts, and we need to hear it from one another. We don't gather because we need more music. We gather because we need more of Christ through one another. I know I can think of many times when I have been encouraged, convicted, and refreshed by singing with the church. We need each other when we sing.

When we view singing as an act of service to one another, we are given even more gospel reasons to sing. Men, your wives and kids need to hear and see you sing. The need to see a leader who unashamedly embraces the truth and emotions the gospel inspires. You are given an awesome opportunity to teach your family the gospel in song. You are given an awesome opportunity to show your son what it looks like to feel powerfully about the gospel. You are given an awesome opportunity to show your daughters that a godly man feels powerfully about the gospel. So sing all the time, as weird as it may feel! Sing around the table, sing on the way to school. Take the opportunity to get the gospel stuck in their heads and hearts.

For those of us who don't feel that we sing well enough, singing as an act of service frees us from the fear of what others will think about our voices. It frees us because we are no longer singing (or not singing) to gain the approval of people. We're singing to share the good news of the gospel with one another. For those of us who struggle with singing based on our preferences or base what church we join on our musical preferences, the gospel frees us to worship God by serving others through our singing.

This is why we sing together, to worship God, and to serve one another. Singing is one of the ways we fulfill what Jesus called the greatest commandment: to love God and love your neighbor as yourself.

REDEEMING THE TIME

Finally, worshipful singing is one of the ways the church learns to "redeem the time." Said another way, how we act as a family shapes how we act when we are out on our own. Think of a newly married couple. They have individually learned all sorts of habits, quirks and expectations from their families, and they bring those to their marriage. For example, in my marriage, my wife and I have conflict over the placement of the hand towel in our kitchen. In my wife's family, they hung the towel over the handle of the oven. In my family, we hung the towel over the counter in front of the kitchen sink. My wife would really prefer it if I would hang the towel over the oven handle. I don't have a preference, but because I am so used to doing it the way I did it growing up, I cannot for the life of me remember to hang it on the oven.

There are millions of different ways we are formed by our biological families. In the same way, we are formed by how we act together as a church family. Singing out of gratefulness to God and in service of one another trains us to live like Christ to the world. It trains and forms us to worship God, to place him at the center of our lives, when we are apart. It builds us up through encouragement, it teaches us through the truth we sing, and it disciplines us for service by giving us ample opportunity to serve one another through song.

Worship is all because of what God has done for us in Christ. We are freed from sin by his life, death, and resurrection. This is what inspires our gratefulness. The gospel of Christ frees us from our fear of man and releases us into serving one another. It frees us from our consumerism, because Christ rightly puts himself at the center of our gatherings and our lives. This is how worship redeems our time—because in our singing, in our gathering, in our service, in our work, in our marriages, in our families, in our hobbies, in our hopes, in our fears, and in our struggles, *God is at the center.*

Because of Christ we have a reason to celebrate. Because of Christ we have hope. Because of Christ we have life. Because of Christ we worship.

22

THANKFULNESS: DEEP, LOUD, AND DANGEROUS
Stephen Witmer

We all know that we should be thankful. Thankfully, the Bible has plenty to say about thankfulness. Among other things, it tells us that thankfulness is deeper, louder, and more dangerous than we might think.

DESIGNED BY GOD
Thankfulness goes much deeper than we might think. It's not a human idea. In fact, it was in the Creator's mind when he created. The Apostle Paul says food was created by God "to be received with thanksgiving by those who believe and know the truth" and then immediately goes on to broaden this out to "everything" God created (1 Tim. 4:3-4). This is a massive theological claim. God created corn on the cob, steak, pasta, avocados (dare we say even Brussels sprouts and liver?) with a specific purpose in mind: that they would be received and then result in thanksgiving flowing back to him. Even a grape and a tangerine can lead a purpose-driven life. Who knew that baby carrots and barbecue ribs and escargot had a *telos*? They do. So do sunsets and flowers and rain, and good conversations and sweet sleep. God intended them to produce thanksgiving. Thankfulness is the God-designed follow-through to God-given blessing.

Giving thanks to God is living along the grain of the universe, savoring God's creation in sync with the Creator. It's one of the very best ways of bringing glory to God (2 Cor. 4:15). On the other hand, enjoying a meal or conversation or movie without feeling thanks to God is a tragic exercise in missing the point. It's a waste, like using a laptop as a paperweight. It's a damaging mistake, like using a light bulb as a hammer.

MEANT TO BE OVERHEARD

Thankfulness can be silent and personal. But very often it ought to be loud enough to be heard by others. Thankfulness wants to point others toward God. And it wants to be a group activity. "Oh, magnify the LORD with me, and let us exalt his name together!" Thankfulness is much happier when someone else can say "amen" (1 Cor. 14:16-17).

In John 11, God (the Son) gives thanks to God (the Father). Jesus stands before the tomb of Lazarus and prays aloud, "Father, I thank you that you have heard me." He then continues praying, stating to God *why* he said just thanks out loud: "I knew that you always hear me, but I said this on account of the people standing around, that they may believe that you sent me." In other words, Jesus gives thanks to God *aloud* because he wants the other people present to overhear his thanksgiving and believe in God and in his mission. That's the whole point. Thankfulness is meant to point others toward God.

In Acts 27, the Apostle Paul is sailing for Rome as a prisoner. The ship he's traveling on gets caught and driven along in a storm for many days, the crew frantically throwing all the cargo overboard. Finally, they approach land and spend a long night in the dark, anchors down. In the morning, here's what happens:

> Paul urged them all to take some food, saying, "Today is the fourteenth day that you have continued in suspense and without food, having taken nothing. Therefore I urge you to take some food. It will give you strength, for not a hair is to perish from the head of any of you." And when he had said these things, he took bread, and giving thanks to God in the presence of all he broke it and began to eat.

I love this little phrase "...and giving thanks to God in the presence of all..." It had been fourteen days since Paul had eaten! He must have been starving. Here was bread in his hands, finally. But he paused and prayed. He gave thanks "in the presence of all," teaching these sailors something about God and about the purpose of food. Paul was living with the grain of the universe, going vertical with thanks, and doing it loud enough for others to hear.

EASILY MISUSED

But thankfulness can be dangerous. It's striking that in the famous story of the Pharisee and the tax collector (Lk. 18:9-14), the one who's recorded as expressing thankfulness is the *Pharisee*. "God, *I thank you* that I am not like other men, extortioners, unjust, adulterers, or even like this tax collector. I fast twice a week; I give tithes of all that I get." Of course, this isn't true thankfulness. True thankfulness is a posture of great humility before God the giver. The Pharisee is using his supposed thankfulness in order to puff himself up. He's taking something designed to make much of God and instead using it to make much of himself. His thankfulness is false cover for his pride. The spotlight operator has turned the spotlight from the stage and is now standing, lit up with ludicrous glory, on the balcony. Pathetic and bizarre. God is clearly not pleased with this perversion of thankfulness. He rejects the Pharisee.

But lest we run too quickly to judgment, have *we* ever used thankfulness amiss? Have we ever publicly thanked God for an accomplishment and in so doing, wished for the accomplishment to be known more than the One we're thanking? Have we ever tweeted "Thankful to God that my new article...my most recent speaking engagement...my kids..." and *mainly* used our thankfulness to announce our latest achievement? Maybe? How easy it is for the spotlight to turn from the stage to the stage hand.

I'm thankful for thankfulness, thankful that God has built it into the fabric of the universe, maximizing both his glory and our joy as we live in sync with his design.

23

THE PRIDEFUL PURSUIT OF HUMILITY
Greg Willson

These days, I have a constant, repetitive prayer to God. One that asks for God to remove my pride and my self-doubt. It's a prayer for humility, something I feel more in need of now than ever before. Pride and self-doubt are really two sides of the same coin. One believes that we know better than God does, the other believes that he isn't good or powerful enough to change us. Neither makes much of God, effectively bringing him down below us. The prideful and the self-doubters both believe they're better than God, they just show it in different ways.

PRIDE AND SELF-DOUBT
Pride is more of an obvious manifestation of a lack of humility. It's easy to spot most of the time. Some of those who struggle with pride link their own lives to their success. And when they don't succeed, it probably wasn't their fault. When things go well, pride points the finger inward; when they don't go well, the finger points outward. Their eyes are horizontal, not vertical.

Self-doubt is a cloaked version of humility's lack. It's not so easy to identify—cynicism can sometimes be seen as merely a need for gentle encouragement. We shouldn't forego being gentle, but a rebuke is also needed for self-doubters. We self-doubters understand well our failures but struggle to see God as more gracious, loving, and forgiving. Essentially, God isn't enough to change us. He doesn't have enough power or goodness. Unlike the prideful, a self-doubter struggles to accept any form of praise. When things go well, their finger points out ward, when they don't, the finger points inward. Again, like the prideful, their eyes are locked horizontally.

Sometimes the prideful are looked up to because of their confidence, albeit broken. Sometimes the self-doubter is looked up to because of their humility, albeit broken. But both really are living lives out of themselves. Neither has "considered the lilies of the field" and looked up to God as provider. One thinks man primarily provides, one denies provision altogether. None asks with the author of Psalm 26, "Test me, O Lord, and try me; examine my heart and mind." One doesn't examine enough; one examines, but without God.

True humility asks the God of the universe to gaze into our-selves with his unflinching eye, that *he* might examine us and illuminate *our shortcomings*. Of course he can do this (and does) on his own without our requests, but there's something impor-tant about that desire coming from us. In our request for God to examine us, there is an implicit acceptance of our faults, the drive to not stay the same, and the belief that God in his good-ness can do something about it.

When confronted with the desire for real humility, we tend to fall into two categories: the anxious and the accepted. The stem of anxiety comes from knowing we're not where we should be, but thinking we can get there on our own. It's a prideful chase of humility. Our eyes are locked towards others or ourselves, never looking up to where our hope comes from.

The stem of acceptance comes from knowing that we are God's beloved children. In Matthew 3:17, Christ is baptized and God declares, "This is my beloved Son, with whom I am well pleased." This same declaration is now directed to those who have faith in Jesus. How can this be? Having faith in Christ means our lives are woven into his. His life becomes our life. His goodness becomes our goodness. Romans 6:4 tells us that Christ's death and his new life become our own. This means it is only by the power of Christ that we can participate in anything like humility. The gospel puts that which is wrong in us to death and brings that which is good to life.

DOING AND BEING

Our doing comes from our being; what we do arises from who we are. And if you are a disciple of Christ, you are, first and foremost, the radically accepted son or daughter of the King. You have flaws and shortcomings, baggage and sins. He has welcome arms. You have brokenness, hurt, pain, and unfulfilled desires. He has a loving embrace.

It is only because of our acceptance with our Father that we can be obedient. Our obedience is our acceptance lived out. And one of the bi-products of this kind of life is humility. It's tricky: searching for humility first attracts pride. But searching after God himself will attract humility. Christ himself embodied this example. Paul teaches us about the Incarnation in Philippians 2:8 and says he "humbled himself." How did Christ do this? By "becoming obedient." Christ, knowing his acceptance in the Trinity, knowing the Father's love towards him, submitted his own body in obedience, in turn bringing about humility. If there was anyone on this earth who could have looked within and mustered their own humility outside of the Father, it would have been Christ. But he was obedient to the Father and that's where Christ's humility shines.

More than merely our example, Christ himself is our means for humility. The Philippians 2:8 passage says that Christ's obedience led to his death, "even death on a cross." Christ's death on the cross was an act for us. Because Christ died, our pride can die. Not because we're good enough, but because Christ has put an end to it. Because Christ died, our self-doubt can die. Not because we're self-effacing, but because Christ looked our sins in the face and took them on, putting them to death. And now, being accepted by our Creator, we can live the new life that Christ rose again for. He walks in resurrection life so that we can. We don't have to be primarily prideful or self-doubting (though we're not perfect... yet), but we can live in the freedom of being an accepted son or daughter of our loving Father.

THE COURAGEOUS SERVANT

Our new freedom takes on the character of a courageous servant. Psalm 116:16 says, "O Lord, I am your servant; I am your servant, the son of your maidservant. You have loosed my bonds." We are not kings, we are servants, not slavishly serving ourselves, but freed to serve the King. Our identity as such does not afford pride. But we servants aren't weak, either. Psalm 31:24 exhorts us to "be strong, and let your heart take courage, all you who wait for the LORD!" We are servants and we are rooted in a strength outside ourselves. This is a vertical orientation.

Both the prideful and the self-doubter need to take courage by waiting on the Lord. If you are tempted to overshadow your inadequacies with pride, take courage. The life you now live is marked by our acceptance by the Father. Run to him, confess, and ask him to change you. If you are tempted to believe that God isn't good enough to change you, run to him, confess, and ask him to change you. This is what waiting on the Lord looks like. This is the obedient life and true humility.

We are saved from pointing the finger inward, saved from pointing the finger outward, freed to live with our hands outstretched heavenward to our loving Father.

24

HOW TO OFFER AND RECEIVE CRITICISM
Mathew B. Sims

Men love not to be judged and censured.
—Richard Sibbes

I have yet to meet the person who enjoys criticism. Whether it's criticism about your work, life, faith, or criticism from an unknown critic online or from a loving family member. All criticism is hard to swallow.

My mom and I have a great relationship. I look back at my formative years and she provided a foundation for the love of God that hasn't left me. I recall the words of Paul to Timothy, "I am reminded of your sincere faith, a faith that dwelt first in your grandmother Lois and your mother Eunice and now, I am sure, dwells in you" (2 Tim. 1:5).

However, I wish I was wiser when hearing her criticism. Her words of encouragement and admonition were coming from a heart of love. Because of my own struggles with hearing criticism, I would often refuse to heed her concerns, only accepting the truth of her words after I'd made a mess of the situation. Hearing criticism is and has been one of the hardest lessons learned in my life, especially if I've received criticism from those whose motives were not in my best interest.

But the gospel should transform the way we give and receive criticism. Today, social networks and blogs have only made it easier to criticize without accountability or real community. It's much easier to make that snarky comment about someone when you don't have to look them in the face.

So, how do we take a gospel-centered approach toward criticism?

THE GOSPEL AND CRITICISM

The gospel transforms the way we receive criticism in four ways. First, it tells us we are created in the image of God. We have value because we are his handiwork, "fearfully and wonderfully made" (Ps. 139:14). What we do has value because we imitate his creativity in creation. None of us is left without a touch of this creativity.

Second, the gospel tells us we are sinful. Charles Spurgeon once said, "If any man thinks ill of you, do not be angry with him; for you are worse than he thinks you to be." Often criticism stings because there may be a teaspoon of truth within the cup of criticism (or maybe a cup of truth within the teaspoon). We know we are sinful. But we almost always give ourselves the benefit of the doubt as we speak, act, and write. It's hard to hear the perspective of someone who may not give us this benefit of the doubt.

Third, the gospel tells us are adopted by God. We have been declared righteous and joined his family and are now being transformed into the image of the Son of God. We are now much more than the sum total of our sins. Criticism can't touch that.

Finally, the gospel tells us that we will be vindicated on the Last Day. George Whitefield reflected, "I am content to wait till the judgement day for the clearing up of my reputation." We should learn to be content now with the righteousness of Christ waiting for our final vindication. For some of us, that might mean allowing our reputation to be tarnished for now.

Scripture actually has much to say about criticism. The following practical suggestions for receiving and giving criticism will hopefully help you build upon these truths.

RECEIVING CRITICISM

1. Hear the Criticism

The writer of Proverbs admonishes us, "Whoever heeds instructions is on the path of life, but he who rejects reproof leads others astray" (Prov. 10:17), "Whoever loves discipline loves knowledge, but he who hates reproof is foolish" (12:1), and "Whoever heeds reproof is prudent" (15:5). These Scriptures only touch the surface. Read through Proverbs for yourself and study what the Solomon teaches about receiving reproof. When criticism is offered, you should hear it, consider it, pray about it, and seek counsel about it. You should also be willing to sift through the criticism for the grain of truth. I have rarely found a criticism where there may not a single grain.

2. Rejoice in the Criticism

Jesus starts one of the greatest sermons ever preached, "Blessed are you when others revile you and persecute you and utter all kinds of evil against you falsely on my account. Rejoice and be glad, for your reward is great in Heaven, for so they persecuted the prophets who were before you" (Matt. 5:11-12).

In this sermon, Jesus addresses criticism that ends up being slanderous lies. Yet he says we are blessed and we should rejoice. How can this be? We are baptized into the body of Christ. We are participants in his life, death, and resurrection. Jesus was persecuted, lied about, and slandered. And the writer of Hebrews says, "[Jesus] who for the joy that was set before him endured the cross, despising the shame, and is seated at the right hand of the throne of God" (Heb. 12:1). This passage connects our joy, suffering, and final vindication by God. Jesus sits at the right hand of God vindicated against the criticism that he made himself to be God (Matt. 26:62-68). We too will stand before God vindicated one day.

3. Compare the Criticism with Scripture.

"All Scripture is breathed out by God and profitable for teaching, for reproof, for correction, and for training in righteousness, that the man of God may be complete, equipped for every good work" (2 Tim. 3:16-17). The truest criticism we will receive comes from Scripture. It speaks honestly about the condition of fallen humanity. Bring the criticism you receive to Scripture and ask the Spirit to uncover truth that might relate to it. Don't miss the full story of the gospel.

4. Don't Respond with Resentment

The worst thing you can do is respond quickly with your own criticism or accusation. But also don't let a "root of bitterness" (Heb. 12:15) take hold in your heart. Resentment will impact you most and the others you love. This last point is especially true when the person clearly doesn't have your best interest in mind and the bulk of their criticism is slander. It's easy to set the record straight about that person, but in my experience that is either almost completely useless because it's peppered with anger or slander in its own right.

OFFERING CRITICISM

1. Be Cautious of Making Accusations

All those who profess Christ are one with Christ. We have been baptized into one body and Spirit (Eph. 4). Christ isn't divided. We should be very careful when criticizing that we aren't accusing another Man's servant (Rom. 14). That doesn't mean we shouldn't take part in polemics, dialogues, debates, and defending the faith. Helpful criticism takes wisdom rooted in Scripture and a robust understanding of how the gospel changes everything.

2. Be Prayerful

Before you ever utter the criticism, pray about it. Ask God for wisdom in using the right words and also that it would be received from a heart of love. Express your dependence on God in sharing this concern with the person. Examine your heart in giving the criticism. If you cannot offer the criticism in good faith (Rom. 14:23) then don't.

3. Seek Peace and Mutual Upbuilding

Paul says, "So then let us pursue what makes for peace and for mutual upbuilding" (Rom. 14:19). I see two connections to the gospel story when see the word "peace." First, peace connects with the Old Testament concept of shalom. It's a state of rest for all of life. In the Old Testament, the shadow was the Promised Land and in the New Testament the fulfillment is the rest we have in Christ. Also, peace is often connected with the blood of Christ and our justification. All of the conflict, rebellion, and sin found in the story of humanity and Israel is resolved when God makes a covenant of peace with Christ (Eph. 2:13-16, 6:14-15; Rom. 5:1-2, and Col. 1:19-20) declaring all those in him as justified and now "fellow heirs with Christ" (Rom. 8:16-17, also see Lk. 2:8-14). The purpose should be to build the hearer up; it shouldn't tear him down. There's correlation with Jesus's instructions for church discipline, the goal of which is restoration.

4. Watch Your Own Life

Paul admonishes the Galatians, "Brothers, if anyone is caught in any transgressions, you who are spiritual should restore him in a spirit of gentleness. Keep watch on yourself lest you too be tempted. Bear one another's burdens, and so fulfill the law of Christ" (Gal. 5:1-2). These instructions are meant to encourage patience, gentleness, and humility. A professor in college who taught counseling would frequently say, "Admonish others as you might expect them to admonish you later." The idea was "today it's me admonishing you; tomorrow it may be you admonishing me." Paul also makes an important point about "bear[ing] one another's burdens." Step in their shoes and understand their struggles. Don't be merciless to those who doubt (Jude 1:22). God doesn't bruise the reed and neither should we. Fan the flame of God's grace in their life.

5. Criticize Sparingly

Paul commands Titus, "As for a person who stirs up division, after warning him once and then twice, have nothing more to do with him" (Titus 3:10). The original context was the local church but there's good application for our personal relationships and online interactions. Depending on the severity of the issue, you may just need to stop criticizing and "have nothing more to do with him." I cannot tell you how tiring it is hearing the same criticism over and over again by the same people about the same person. It takes wisdom to understand at what point you are casting your pearls before the swine (Matt. 7:6).

It's important to search Scripture when understanding how to receive and give criticism. The Internet has made it easy to register our criticisms and provides a platform for those with grudges. These interactions are front and center for the world to see. We must learn to interact in a way which glorifies God. "Do you not know that we are to judge angels? How much more, then, matters to pertaining to this life!" (1 Cor. 6:3).

25

DOUBT IS NOT A DISEASE
Matt Manry

Should we focus on engaging those who are skeptical about the truths of Christianity? Should Christians who are struggling with their faith join a discipleship group? Should the Church spend more time and resources engaging the doubts that people have in regards to Jesus Christ?

Well, yes.

Tim Keller said:

> A faith without some doubts is like a human body with no antibodies in it. People who blithely go through life too busy or indifferent to ask the hard questions about why they believe as they do will find themselves defenseless against either the experience of tragedy or the probing questions of a smart skeptic. A person's faith can collapse almost overnight if she failed over the years to listen patiently to her own doubts, which should only be discarded after long reflection.

Keller makes it clear that in today's world, we must be willing to acknowledge the doubts that we have and to confront them. Sometimes evangelicals tend to overlook the doubts that people struggle with and just sweep them under the rug. This is not the solution. Church leaders must focus on discipling those who are struggling with doubt. Here is what Scripture reveals to us about faith and doubt.

FAITH IS A GIFT

In Romans 12:3 the Apostle Paul says, "For by the grace given to me I say to every-one among you not to think of himself more highly than he ought to think, but to think with sober judgment, each according to the measure of faith that God has assigned." As we meditate on this verse, we are able to see that God gives out different amounts of faith to his people. The measure and amount of one's faith depends totally on what God has assigned. Faith is a gracious gift from God. However, we are also able to see that doubt is a tool that our Father in Heaven uses for his purposes and plans. In God's sovereignty, he sometimes uses doubt as a tool to drive us to Jesus Christ. All of this is done in his perfect timing. With that framework in mind, we can now turn our attention to examining why doubt should not be taboo.

Scripture reveals many doubters to us. The disciple, Thomas, is probably most widely known for struggling with doubt (Jn. 20:24-29). However, there are plenty of others who are worth mentioning. Abraham struggled with believing that God could make him a father in his old age (Gen. 17:17). Moses did not believe God could use him to bring the children of Israel out of Egypt (Exod. 3:10-15). Peter struggled with belief, when he almost drowned at sea (Matt. 14:28-32). So if you struggle with doubt, know you are not alone. The Bible is full of doubters who were used by God for his sovereign purposes, and there is no question he can use those who struggle with doubt today.

There are plenty of men and women you probably know who struggle with doubt within your church. These people should not be treated as inferior Christians. They should not be treated as people who have an infectious disease. When we understand that faith is a gift and that the measure of one's faith does not determine the level of one's spiritual maturity, we will finally be a people who do not drive doubters away from the church. The church should always be a place for skeptics and saints alike.

If all of us were honest with ourselves we would admit that doubting as a Christian is not abnormal. When Christians go through intense trials or have been praying for God to answer a specific prayer over a prolonged period of time with no answer, doubts arise. Does this suggest they are not trusting God enough? Perhaps not. I have found myself more than once in my life exclaiming in prayer the same words uttered by the father of a demon possessed child (Mk. 9:21-24). The simple prayer: "I believe; help my unbelief" is indeed a prayer that should be included in almost every Christian's life.

The reason this prayer should be included in our prayer life is because of the ever-present reality that Christians struggle with doubt. This should not make us feel ashamed. We must always remember that Jesus Christ still heals the child in Mark 9 despite his father's doubt. This should encourage us because it serves as a constant reminder that God still works with us and in us through our doubts.

Picture yourself in a home group filled with both skeptics and mature believers. Imagine the diversity of this group. Skeptics are able to voice their concerns and ask questions about the faith. Mature believers are able to evangelize and present the gospel message in a practical way. This benefits both parties and there is no question that a community like this would encourage skeptics and believers.

THE GOSPEL FOR DOUBT

There is good news for those who are struggling with doubt—the gospel. The good news proclaims to both skeptics and saints that God has done everything for us through Christ Jesus. His faith excels where our faith falters. Unbelievers and believers should acknowledge their doubts and always be willing to confront them head on. The church can help in this area. The gospel is the message that the church should always proclaim because it is the only message that has enough power to provide confidence for both the unbeliever and the believer.

An unbeliever might be struggling with doubting certain tenets of Christianity, and he might need to be confronted with an apologetic defense of the faith, but that should never take complete place over the gospel message. Hearing the gospel proclaimed is what leads to faith (Rom. 10:17). For a believer, the gospel is what encourages the Christian to look to Jesus Christ and his finished work even in the midst of doubts. Christians must preach the gospel to themselves because it serves as an antidote for the doubtful heart and mind.

The Church should always do everything it can do to help those who are struggling with doubt. There are various ways that this could be done, but I believe that the most effective way is by explicitly and constantly proclaiming the good news of what Christ Jesus has done for sinners.

And we must always remember that faith is a gift, and doubt is not a disease.

26

THE DANGER OF NOT DOUBTING
Nick Rynerson

"Who is Jesus?" I asked students on the first day of class.

"The son of God"

"God"

"The Savior"

They concluded drearily between secretly checking their smart phones and staring vacantly at me, as if I were speaking Portuguese. So I ask again, "Really, who is Jesus?" If you had walked into the classroom, you would've assumed we were practicing our awkward silences.

I used to teach Bible classes at a nice little Christian high school with about sixty students and a fairly conservative culture. They're good kids. Most of them are remarkably bright and incredible at Bible trivia. But something was missing.

The students, like most students, have been taught to memorize and regurgitate information. They are actually pretty good at it. And my students have had the added blessing of memorizing and regurgitating incredible biblical truths on a daily basis for most of their lives. But there is, for the most part, a lack of any realization that the biblical truths they are memorizing are actually true!

I believe their apathy (and all apathy) is rooted in deep doubts about the goodness, practicality, and truth of the information they're being taught. In high school, I hated math because I doubted its usefulness and I didn't trust Old Man Marley for the first half of *Home Alone* because I thought he was secretly a bad guy.

I believe a lot of these students have doubts about who God is, why they have to read the Bible, and what the "good news of Jesus Christ" has to do with anything. Not because they weren't raised in godly Christian homes, or because they are rebels—because they are human. Humans doubt truth. We always have.

EVERYDAY DOUBT

When we approach the profound truths of God or anything, really, sometimes we just see a black hole—something that seems impossible to comprehend, enjoy, or believe. We doubt every day. Every time we fear the unknown, we practice doubt.

We cannot just ignore or write off doubt. We must wrestle with it.

Belief is essential in the Christian life. John wrote his account of the life, death, and resurrection "so that [we] may believe that Jesus is the Christ, the Son of God, and that by believing you may have life in his name" (Jn. 20:31). Paul says that grace comes to us "through faith" (Eph. 2:8). And Jesus says that the work of God is to believe in Jesus!

But belief isn't easy. Belief is not simply scoring high marks on a Bible quiz. It's the pursuit of truth, an investigation into the depths of reality. As Jonathan Dodson says in *Raised?*,

> Anything worth believing has to be worth questioning, but don't let your questions slip away unanswered. Don't reduce your doubts to a state of unsettled cynicism. Wrestle with your doubts. Find answers. If you call yourself a believer don't settle for pat proofs, emotional experiences, or duty-driven religion. Keep asking questions.

My students had been catechized well, but they had never wrestled with their doubts, and in turn most have never interacted with the living Jesus. They assume that expressing doubts will get them in trouble but really, they will be in much deeper trouble if they never ask what it means. Despite what they may think, their doubts may, in fact, be from God.

Just as God came down from Heaven to wrestle with (not to catechize!) Jacob (Gen. 32), doubts may at first seem to be an enemy, but prove to be dear friends. As George MacDonald observed,

> Doubts are the messengers of the Living One to the honest. They are the first knock at our door of things that are not yet, but have to be, understood...Doubt must precede every deeper assurance; for uncertainties are what we first see when we look into a region hitherto unknown, unexplored, unannexed.

Don't fear doubting. Our doubts can take us deeper into the knowledge of God, not further away. When we wrestle with God, we come away changed.

So I began to encourage doubt in my classroom. While I still taught my students the fundamentals theology and mission, I wanted to teach them to wrestle with God. I wanted them to ask the hard questions—to really ask themselves (and me), "What does this mean?" The process was often long and arduous, but as a student once wrote on a worksheet, "If you don't ask questions, you won't get answers."

USING DOUBT IN DISCIPLESHIP

How can we steward doubt—"messengers of the Living One to the honest"—in the already messy process of disciple-making? I don't know exactly, but here are five general thoughts on disicpling amidst doubt.

1. Don't Ignore Doubt

Have the courage to look for doubt. When someone gives a "Sunday school" answer, don't be afraid to search for the heart behind the answer. Maybe there is a true, orthodox love for God behind that "right answer," but that isn't always the case. Jesus didn't ignore Thomas's doubt—he directly engaged it. Jesus didn't condemn him for his doubt, but told him,

"Put your finger here, and see my hands; and put out your hand, and place it in my side. Do not disbelieve, but believe." Thomas answered him, "My Lord and my God!" (Jn. 20:28)

2. Be Humble

Just because you don't wrestle with nagging doubts (right now) doesn't mean that the doubts of others are not legitimate. Pride is particularly deadly when you are instructing others. Humbly encourage doubters to draw from the same well of truth you have. This will foster a safe environment for others as they wrestle with their doubts.

3. See Doubt as an Opportunity

Doubt can certainly lead to sin, but doubt can be an opportunity to trust and seek God. Encourage yourself and others to "see doubt as the door to that which is unknown, but must be known." Faith is not the absence of doubt, but the "assurance of things hoped for, the conviction of things not seen" (Heb. 11:1). God can, and historically has, used honest doubts as an opportunity to lead believers to rest, repent, and believe. Doubt is an opportunity to encounter the living truth, and, as Sir Francis Bacon observed, "No pleasure is comparable to the standing upon the vantage ground of truth."

4. Remember the Gospel

The absolutely certain, imputed, and active righteousness of Christ shows us our doubt is not our demise. Doubts do not stop God from saving, loving, and pursuing his people! This means that when a brother or sister in Christ is wrestling through doubts—intellectual or otherwise—God still loves them. He still views them as perfectly hidden in Christ. The cross is doubt-proof; as much as we doubt, we cannot change the glorious, historical truth that Jesus died once for sin. This means that every question is safe to ask and no doubt is too big for the cross to overcome. Jesus's perfect lack of doubt has overcome our doubt.

5. Remember that God Transforms Doubt

Thankfully, God does not leave doubters in their doubt. God has a long record of intervening in human history and radically transforming even the strongest doubters. From Moses (Exod. 3) to Job to Jonah to Thomas, God works through those who have deep doubts about God and their call. Consider Sarah:

> The Lord said, "I will surely return to you about this
> time next year, and Sarah your wife shall have a son."
> And Sarah was listening at the tent door behind him.
> Now Abraham and Sarah were old, advanced in years.
> The way of women had ceased to be with Sarah. So
> Sarah laughed to herself, saying, "After I am worn out,
> and my lord is old, shall I have pleasure?" (Gen.
> 18:9-12)

God promised things that seemed impossible. Our humanness wants to doubt God because, honestly, some of the things God promises are insane. But God delivers. Sarah laughed at the thought that God could ever fulfill his promises, but God answered Sarah's doubts and through it, glorified himself,

> The Lord visited Sarah as he had said, and the Lord did
> to Sarah as he had promised. And Sarah conceived and
> bore Abraham a son in his old age at the time of which
> God had spoken to him. Abraham called the name of
> his son who was born to him, whom Sarah bore him,
> Isaac. And Abraham circumcised his son Isaac when
> he was eight days old, as God had commanded
> him. Abraham was a hundred years old when his son
> Isaac was born to him. And Sarah said, "God has made
> laughter for me; everyone who hears will laugh over
> me. (Gen. 21:1-7)

Sarah's laughter was transformed from doubt to joy. God answered Sarah and God answers our doubts. God replaces our doubt with worship. The burden of proof is on God, and God comes though. This was the only hope I had that my high school students would encounter God in the foolishness of my teaching.

CONCLUSION

We never "arrive" and we will never know everything. As long as sin wages war against the Spirit, we will struggle with doubts. But thankfully, we are not alone in this struggle. Our perfect righteousness, hidden in Christ, is secure despite our doubts. And God has promised to be with us in our fight with doubt. My students didn't "get the gospel" immediately. They often played Flappy Bird in class instead of wrestling with truth. But as Jonathan Dodson rightfully notes in *Raised?*,

> Those who are skeptical and struggling with belief, Jesus remains ready to receive your questions. He will listen to your doubts.

MULTIPLY
DISCIPLES

27

THE GOSPEL AND THE GREAT COMMANDMENT
Abe Meysenburg

In Matthew 28, Jesus made it clear that an integral part of discipleship is "teaching them to obey all that I have commanded you." And if you're going to teach someone to obey all that Jesus commanded, you might as well start with the most important commandment. In Matthew 22:36-40, Jesus engaged in a conversation with a Pharisee who asked:

> "Teacher, which is the great commandment in the Law?" And he said to him, "You shall love the Lord your God with all your heart and with all your soul and with all your mind. This is the great and first commandment. And a second is like it: You shall love your neighbor as yourself. On these two commandments depend all the Law and the Prophets."

How much of our disciple-making effort revolves around this simple (but difficult) command to love God? Do we begin with this command? Do we emphasize it enough? In the lives of those whom we are discipling, do we ask questions concerning love for God?

As with every command in Scripture, the gospel should be the ultimate motivator compelling us to obedience. Clearly the gospel encompasses much more than the doctrine of the love of God, but for the purposes of this discussion, I'll encapsulate the meaning of "the gospel" with the phrase "he loved us" from 1 John 4:10: "This is love: not that we loved God, but that he loved us and sent his Son as an atoning sacrifice for our sins."

HE LOVES US

God loves us. The very thought should take our breath away. God loves us, and that love has ultimately resulted in Jesus exchanging our sin for his righteousness. The Scriptures declare,

> "But God demonstrates his love for us, in that, while we were yet sinners, Christ died for us." (Rom. 5:8)

> "In love he predestined us for adoption as sons." (Eph. 1:5)

> "Because of his great love for us, God, who is rich in mercy, made us alive with Christ." (Eph. 2:4-5)

God loves us. God loves us. He loves us! The initial (and inevitable) response to this love is reciprocal love for God.

An increased focus on gospel-centrality is extremely instructive in helping us correct our wrong actions. We discover that our wrong actions are driven by wrong beliefs. When we sin, we understand that we are not believing the gospel. We become familiar with Luther's observation about the Ten Commandments: if you break #2 through #10, it's because you broke #1 first. This is true and helpful.

However, those of us who swim in the waters of gospel-centrality have not always done a great job of pointing out the positive effects of believing the gospel. I know that when I sin, I'm not believing the gospel, but what should it look like when *I am* believing the gospel? At the risk of sounding ridiculously simple, I believe the answer is: love God.

When I truly, deeply believe the gospel, I will love God. I will be filled with gratitude and joy, a gratitude that has a direction (Godward) and that joy will have an object (God). The gospel propels me to say, "God, I love you!"

LOVING OBEDIENCE

On the heels of that declaration will come the express desire to obey: "If you love me, you will keep my commands." Being awash in the love of God elicits a pledge of devotion, a glad desire to obey the Father. We respond, "God, I love you and want to do whatever you say."

Is there a clearer example of this than Jesus himself? Everything Jesus did was motivated by his love for the Father. Disciples walk in the ways of Jesus. This involves not only right actions, but right motives. It was love for God that drove Jesus to pray, "Not my will, but yours be done." God, I love you and want to do whatever you say!

And his first marching order for us has already been issued—love God. Love others, the second most important command according to Jesus, follows. In some ways (and again, at the risk of sounding ridiculously simple), this command encompasses the rest of life. Shouldn't everything we do be motivated by love for God primarily and love for people secondarily? Can you think of anything you would do, prompted by the Spirit, that would not somehow benefit another person?

Whether you are teaching or counseling or sending email or cooking dinner or returning phone calls or doing laundry or running errands or pursuing a spouse or writing a blog post, your motive should be love for God. We respond, "God, in response to what you have done for me, I declare my love for you. I engage in this activity for you. I love you, and want to obey you."

So when the single men in our community want to pursue a girl, I remind them to do it primarily because they love God and want to obey him. This keeps the whole endeavor about God and not about the girl. I'll ask, "Do you believe the Father is leading you to do this? Is your motive to love and obey him? Is your motive to bless her as a sister regardless of her response?"

Or when a young leader is discouraged because the people in his missional community are not responding, I'll remind him that he leads because he loves God, not because he expects a particular response from the people he's leading. Obviously, we pray and hope for a response, but we don't lead only so people will respond. We lead because we love (and we love because he loves us). "If I speak with the tongues of men and of angels but have not love, I am a noisy gong or a clanging cymbal" (1 Cor. 13:1).

If our motivation in any area of life—work, marriage, parenting, or leadership—is connected to an expected outcome, then we are actually serving ourselves and not other people. We are using them to get something we want (power, position, acceptance, love, etc.). Only when we serve out of love for God can we truly love people.

Perhaps this is why Jesus said that love for God and love for people were the most important commandments. What more important commandments could we encourage a disciple to obey? And what a better way to live a life in response to the gospel than to love God and love others!

Let the gospel (he loves us) be the motive (love God) for all that we do (love others).

28

Fighting Against Mission Fatigue
Brad Watson

Over the last month, in communities and organizations across the spectrum of the gospel-centered missional movement, I have come across a growing number of people on the cusp of burnout. Many were close friends, a few were acquaintances, and at least one of them was me. Tired, worn out souls exhausted from community and mission. They are faithful people; well trained, well supported, and well resourced. What's worse, their exhaustion with the mission usually coincides with financial, marital, and familial stress.

CAUSES OF MISSION FATIGUE
So, what is going on? As a child of this movement, I have often been at a loss. I thought we had it covered? We are supposed to center our lives on the gospel and then live intentional and communal lives empowered by the Spirit, making disciples of Jesus. If this was the plan, why does it keep spitting out exhausted and discouraged people? It wasn't until I personally stared this burnout in the face and searched my soul that I discovered why the gospel mission has become the exhausted mission.

1. Looking for the Wrong Fruit
We are looking for fruit. We desire fruitful lives. In my own journey, as the months and years continued to pass by without a rapid multiplication of communities with baptisms and new churches formed, I grew exhausted and discouraged. We must

be doing something wrong! I must be doing something wrong! Eventually, I simply thought that I had wasted years of my life. I was fruitless. Many of the people I talk to experiencing missional exhaustion have the same experience. Interestingly, the fruit that is expected from us in the Scriptures, not in our heads, is not new churches, converts, or communities. Rather, God wants to produce love, peace, patience, kindness, goodness, gentleness, and self-control in us (Gal 5:22-25).

God wants to produce love, peace, patience, kindness, goodness, gentleness, and self-control in us.

On the other side, this is what the Spirit does through us: performs miracles, brings people to repentance and faith, produces new life, gives gifts, baptizes, and appoints elders, among other things. Leaders experience discouragement when we measure the wrong things. When you strive to produce things that the Spirit is in charge of, you work harder than you ought and place responsibility on yourself that you could never carry. This is a sure recipe for exhaustion.

However, when we pause and reflect on the fruit of the Spirit born in us, we are encouraged because we see things the way we are. When I stopped to see the things the Spirit had done in me, I realized my life wasn't fruitless. In fact, it had been very fruitful. Over the years God had given me love for people I didn't even know at the beginning. God had given me peace in my heart and marriage. God had created, seemingly out of nothing, a contentment with small budgets and his presence. The reality was, God had been working in me. Ironically, it was that fruit in me that God used to produce fruit in others.

2. Living with an Urgency of Ego

Leaders who are striving for success and 'great stories' expect them to happen immediately. This is one of the oldest tricks the enemy uses to destroy mission: get them to think we can make a name for themselves. The urgency to have a thriving missional community or life that produces results that are celebrated is exhausting. It is tiring trying to be an expert and gain the affections of 'missional' peers. Self-serving mission leads to burnout 100% of the time. If the urgency of ego isn't for self-gain, it is for another's. I have also witnessed people crushed by the burden of proving themselves to their leaders' apparent expectations, which many cases, didn't exist.

3. Living with an Urgency of Ideal

This is a slightly different urgency. This is where the goal is to do exactly what we read in the 'book' or saw at the conference. We expect and strive to do things by the book. The books are helpful and so are the conference speakers. What becomes exhausting is a newfound legalism—modalism. When you have a problem or get stuck, you are turning to the expert's blog, book, twitter feed, and videos. These can be helpful, no doubt. But in the end, the mission is too difficult to look for strength and endurance in a model that can't offer either.

The mission is too difficult to look for strength and endurance in a model that can't offer either.

4. Agenda-filled Relationships

When every relationship you have comes with an 'intentional' and strategic plan to make them a disciples of Jesus, you run out of steam quickly—because you don't have any relationships. Every holiday, season, sporting event, and errand has become 'intentional' in all the wrong ways. Agenda-driven intentionality is: "What can I do for God in these things?" Or worse: "How can I move this person one step closer to buying into my belief system?" To be clear, I am all for intentionality and I completely agree that God is using us and can use us all the time. However, I would add that God *wants* to do something in us at all times. Gospel intentionality, the opposite of agenda-driven intentionality, asks regularly: "What is God doing, where is he, what is he saying?" Or, better yet: "What can I do to see him clearly in all of life?" The gospel means we are reconciled with Christ. Our redemption is to life with him. Our commission is with him.

We often forget this in our rush to live intentional and missional lives. We aren't trying to figure out how to make disciples all the time. Rather, we are trying experience Jesus in every part of life. Discipleship is inviting people to experience the reconciliation and redemption of Jesus in their lives, too. In this way, be a normal person who experiences the supernatural presence of Jesus through the power of the Holy Spirit.

5. Lack of Patience

We often expect to see fully-formed disciples after a few months or even a few years. When we don't, we throw our hands up and say, "This doesn't work, what else can I try?" Imagine you move into a street where your house is the only one that believes Jesus is King and Savior of the world, and even you struggle to believe it in almost every area of life. However, you buckle down and go for it. After a few years, you have made great relationships with neighbors and have spoken the gospel in several ways and at several moments. You have wrestled with some of your idols, too. Your marriage went through a very difficult time, but you are starting to see restoration. You praise God for all your new friends, opportunities, and growth. But you feel that you have failed. You haven't baptized anyone. You should stop what you are doing.

6. Bad Math

If you attempt to do more than you are called or asked of by Jesus, you will be tired. There is a simple equation found in the book *Margin* by Richard Swenson: Your Load (or what you are called to do)–Your Power = Margin.

Your load is what you are called to do, what is being asked of you, what you have taken on as your responsibility. Your power is your capacity, gifts, time, strength, and finance at your disposal to do it. Margin is either sanity or chaos, under- or over-utilization. It is a simple equation: if you are committed beyond your power, you will be exhausted. If you do far less than you have power to do, you will be bored. Too often, we assume the role of saving the planet or at the least our community. We accept great and worthwhile roles and responsibilities followed by a belief that we are omnipresent, omniscient, and omnipotent. If you don't believe you are those things, you have believed the laws of time, finances, and energy don't apply to you. You press on with a packed schedule and slim bank account. The Spirit is powerful and works in remarkable ways.

The Spirit does not call you to more than he will supply the power. Jesus calls us to more than we can do on our own, but he doesn't call us to more than he will empower.

Simple prayers and questions: What is Jesus giving me power for? What is Jesus asking me to do?

7. Mission-Centered

Finally, at the end of the day, if we are not gospel-centered, we cannot be mission-centered. The noblest idol in all of Christianity is mission. We approve when people worship it, celebrate it, and lay their life down for it. The idol of converts is as powerful as it is subtle. It is easy to drift. Here lies the problem: mission doesn't give power, energy, grace, or redemption. Reconciliation of the gospel makes us ambassadors for the Reconciler, not mini-reconcilers. This is the end result of all the things mentioned above.

We have drifted from gospel-centered life to a mission-centered life. When this happens, we make disciples of the mission instead of disciples of Jesus.

FIGHTING FATIGUE

We are susceptible to mission fatigue. The question is, what are we supposed to do about it?

1. Repent

If you are believing and living any of the things above, you are worshiping false gods, telling God you are a better missionary than the Spirit and a better savior than Jesus. You've made the mission of God your god. Turn from those things and toward the true God:

- The God who is great, so do you don't have to be in control of the mission.
- The God who is good, so you don't have to look to the mission for personal satisfaction.
- The God who is glorious, so you don't have to look for significance in the mission.

- The God who is gracious, so you don't have to prove yourself in the mission.

This is the God who invites you to join him on his mission; the God who infinitely cares for you. What practices remind you of that truth?

2. Live in the Urgency of Spirit
God is patient. Somehow we think that the Spirit is frantic and urgent, but he is actually patient and powerful. Consider the lame man healed by the Spirit in Acts 3. This man had to have been passed by Jesus multiple times in his life. Somehow God waited to heal the man much later. Or consider the decades of patience as the gospel slowly moved into Europe and only after a dream appeared to Paul after days of being denied by the Spirit. The Holy Spirit is not a yes man. The Holy Spirit waits, says no, prepares, and works over time as much as he works in an instance.

3. Seek Rhythms of Rest
Finally, learn to rest regularly. First, learn what rest means. Rest does not mean doing nothing. Rest also doesn't mean doing chores around the house. Rest also doesn't mean 'family time.' All of those things may be components of rest for you. However, rest truly means to marvel at all the God has done and is doing. The first day in the life of a human was not building, organizing, it was resting in the goodness God had created. It was only after that day of resting in God and what he had done did we go to work doing the things he commanded them to do. We live on mission from a starting point of rest. We don't rest from the mission, we get on mission because we rest.

We don't rest from the mission, we get on mission because we rest.

This means that you learn how to remember and worship the goodness of God. Make space within your life to focus on resting in God's work. You will do this daily. You will do this weekly. You will do this monthly, seasonally, and annually. These are patterns throughout the Old Testament with sabbaths, festivals, and jubilees. In each of these, people stopped trying to make things happen. They left their fields, their military posts, their labor, etc. The point was always to remember and celebrate the things that God had done to redeem them and form them into a people. It is good wisdom for us to do the same. What does this look like? My example:

- Daily, I take a 15-minute walk through my neighborhood praying and reflecting on what God had done the day before. Asking him on that day, "Help me see you and step into the things you call me into."
- Weekly, I take a day where I intentionally focus on what God is doing and has done. I remember the gift of him. For me, I journal, write, read, and spend time with my family. We remind me of grace. We also spend time with friends and neighbors on this day. However, the point of this day is to celebrate and worship who God is and what he has done.
- Monthly, I get out of town or at the minimum my neighborhood. I read, write, and mostly pray. I've found a monastery an hour and a half away and the drive alone is worth it. Also, at different times in our marriage, my wife and I have been able to spend a night out of our context once a month. This is an amazing practice everyone should try. As we leave, we pray and ask God to bless our time. While we are away we reflect on the past month.
- Annually, I take a real vacation, even if it is a staycation. During this week or so, do what is relaxing and enjoyable to you. Hike, ski, swim, sun bath, read, whatever is enjoyable. Eat good food and listen to good music. Reflect and worship God for what he has done and pray for the things you hope God will do in the next year.

As you do all of these enjoyable things of rest, take time to reflect on these questions:

- What were the low-lights and hard things last year?
- What were the high-lights and clear blessings last year? (Oddly, these answers end up being the same as the hard things.)
- What did we see God doing last year?
- What do we hope to see happen this next year?
- What fruit do we pray to see this next year?
- What are our fears with this next year?
- How is God good, great, glorious, and gracious?

THE BEST WAY TO SPEND YOUR LIFE

I want to leave you with an appeal. Do not leave a life on mission because you have made it the entirety of your life. There is a way to be on mission and for your life to be about Jesus. In fact, this is the only sustainable way. As you press into seeing Jesus present, involved, and relevant at your dinner table, at work, in the garden, and with your friends, you will be on mission. The gospel is the only agent of perseverance. This is one thrilling life of repentance, faith, and fruit.

Jesus is worth it! You will find Jesus on the mission, but don't substitute the mission for Jesus.

29

HOW JESUS MADE DISCIPLES
Winfield Bevins

What you have heard from me in the presence of many witnesses
entrust to faithful men who will be able to teach others also.
—2 Timothy 2:2

Many Christians and churches will never reproduce themselves. The result is that they take their faith and legacy with
them to the grave. Nearly four thousand churches close every
year in North America. Ed Stetzer estimates that 70% to 80% of
all evangelical churches in the U.S. have either stopped growing
or are in decline! What does this mean? Simple: the church in
North America must not be reproducing. We need to become a
reproducing disciple-making movement.

The ultimate goal of discipleship is to reproduce disciples
with the gospel through developing disciple making leaders and
church planting. Reproduction ensures that a movement will
live past its founding stages. The church was never intended to
be an end in itself; rather it is called to reproduce and fulfill the
Great Commission to make disciples. Reproduction is the goal of
every living thing. We see this throughout the pages of the Bible. The Bible is full of reproductive language. God created hu-
mankind, animals, and plants to reproduce. Reproduction is
also seen in the agricultural language that Jesus uses throughout the Gospels.

Reproducing disciples is the result of selecting, training,
and empowering leaders who will in turn reproduce themselves in others. This begins locally with the church and then
can take place on a larger scale through reproduction of church

plants regionally and internationally. You can be a part of a 21st century disciple making movement that can change our postmodern world for Christ.

REPRODUCING DISCIPLES: A FEW GOOD MEN *AND* WOMEN

The most powerful paradigm for reproducing disciples is the discipleship methodology of Jesus. In *The Master Plan of Evangelism*, Robert Coleman tells us that Jesus's plan of reproducing disciples, "was not with programs to reach the multitudes but with men whom the multitudes would follow...Men were to be his method of winning the world to God. The initial objective of Jesus's plan was to enlist men who could bear witness to his life and carry on his work after he returned to the Father." If we are to be like Jesus, we must invest our lives in faithful men and women who will reproduce themselves in others.

Coleman's *book* offers the following eightfold way Jesus trained the twelve disciples; selection, association, consecration, impartation, demonstration, delegation, supervision, and reproduction. In this section, I will summarize Coleman's analysis of Jesus training of the twelve disciples in this section and apply it to reproducing disciples.

1. Selection

It all started when Jesus called a few men to follow him. Jesus did not choose everyone he met to be his disciples. He took very seriously the selection of men he trained. Rather than focusing on the multitude, he only chose twelve. The reason for his selectivity was intentional. He chose twelve men and a number of women to instruct and train. They would in time reproduce themselves in others. A few good men and women were Jesus's master plan of reproducing disciples.

In a similar way, we must be selective in the people with whom we choose to disciple. We should look for people who are faithful, willing, and able to reproduce their discipleship in others. Disciple making does not require a degree or Bible college education; rather we should seek to find men and women who have a passion and a hunger to for Christ. Willingness to answer the call to follow Jesus is the only requirement to be a disciple of Jesus.

2. Association

Jesus was intimately involved in the lives of his disciples as they followed him. His training method was spending time with his disciples. Coleman points out that Jesus had no formal training or education; he was his own school and curriculum. This is a radical concept for those of us who live in the 21st century. Whenever we find someone, who seems called into ministry we send them off to let someone else train them. The New Testament model of discipleship was homegrown, natural, and organic. Discipleship happens as men and women spend time with their spiritual mentor.

In a similar way, we should be in the lives of the people we are seeking to develop. We should schedule time with people who we want to disciple outside of normal church functions. We should schedule times to play, pray, and share a meal together with the people we are discipling. This means that discipleship will require something of us. Discipleship costs us something even for those of us who are called to disciple others. We must sacrifice our time, energy, and emotion in others if we are to fulfill the discipleship task of making disciples. I believe this is one of the number one reasons that churches don't disciple anymore. It takes "too much" time.

3. Consecration

Jesus expected his followers to obey him. He sought to create in his disciples a lifestyle of consecrated obedience. Discipleship is about a total consecration to the Lord. As disciples, we need to submit and obey God's word and plan for our lives. However, many of us have trouble submitting. We live in an individualistic culture where people do not want anyone else telling us what to do. That is why submission and obedience to God is so hard as well as important. When we become obedient to God in every area of our lives, we will experience victorious Christian living. God can only use men and women who are willing to obey him.

4. Impartation

Jesus gave himself away to his disciples by imparting to them everything that the Father had given him. He gave himself freely. He imparted not only himself, but also spiritual truth about life and ministry. He taught them about the Scriptures and the Holy Spirit. Just as Jesus imparted himself to his disciples, we must seek to give ourselves to the men and women that we are called to serve. There is a transfer of godly wisdom and character when true discipleship takes place. As leaders, it is important for us to grasp that we have a spiritual responsibility to impart ourselves in others if we are going to make disciples.

5. Demonstration

Jesus demonstrated how the disciples should live the Christ-centered life. One reason Jesus had such a lasting impact on his disciples is that he lived the message before them daily. He was the message and the method. By walking with Jesus, they saw how he lived his faith in the real world. He prayed before them. He fed the poor. He had compassion on the multitude. He healed the sick. In other words, he lived the life that he wanted to reproduce in his disciples. After Jesus's death and resurrection, he expected his disciples to say and do what he said and did.

It is important that we practice what we preach, because the people we are training will follow our life and example. It is not enough to preach the gospel, we have to practice it daily. Our personal walk with God is one of the most important factors in developing godly leaders. We will reproduce what we are. The most powerful message is a life lived for God. Make sure that the life you live is worthy for others to follow.

6. Delegation

Jesus assigned his disciples work. He developed his disciples by delegating ministry responsibilities to them. He sent his disciples out and gave them hands-on experience. This was a vital part of Jesus's discipleship curriculum. It's funny that churches make people do things even Jesus did not do. Some churches make people go through a yearlong process before they can serve in any capacity in the church. Likewise, some people spend years in college and seminary with little if any real ministry involvement.

Churches need to rethink delegating spiritual responsibility to people, especially new believers. Is it any wonder our discipleship is often anemic? Sadly, most people think the pastor is supposed to do everything in the church. We must not forget the power of involving people in ministry.

7. Supervision

Supervision is important. Jesus supervised his disciples. Whenever they returned from a ministry trip, they would report to him. This allowed a time for the disciples to reflect, review, and to receive instruction from Jesus. Supervision is an important part of leadership development, especially when dealing with new believers. We want to delegate and empower people to act, but we also need to help supervise them to make sure they stay on track. Many times people will get into trouble without proper supervision. Supervision is an art. On the one hand, if we are not careful, we can micro-manage people. On the other hand, we can be so loose that we don't supervise people at all.

8. Reproduction

Jesus expected his disciples to reproduce his likeness in others. He imparted his message and mission to his disciples so that they would reproduce themselves in others and make disciples of all nations. The Great Commission implies that the followers of Jesus will reproduce themselves and "make disciples." Reproduction is how the Christian movement was born.

Today, what has become a 2.1 billion-member movement started with only twelve disciples. I want to return to the analogy of the vine in John 15:1-17. The purpose of the vine (Jesus) and the branches (Christians) is to bear fruit. Christians are to work for and expect a harvest (Matt. 9:37-38; Lk. 10:2). Let us commit our lives and our churches to reproducing ourselves in others in order to make disciples of our communities and our world.

We need to rediscover the reproductive nature of the church. We are called to select, train, and send missional disciples of Christ out into the world who will be able repeat the process of discipleship. What we need in our day is an organic disciple making movement that will train and send men and women to be reproducing disciples of Christ.

30

THE UNQUALIFIED DISCIPLE
Lindsay Fooshee

When I ask women in our church if they would be willing to invest in a discipleship relationship with a younger woman, I am usually met with hesitation. "Me?" their eyes seem to ask. "Me? Disciple someone else? You must not really know me. I don't think I'm qualified."

The conversations take different forms, but the responses are often the same. Again and again, I hear women voice a sincere doubt that they have anything worthwhile to give. Even if they are willing to give a discipleship relationship a try, deep down they are thinking with something akin to panic, "I've got nothing!" Surely this isn't just a women's problem. Every disciple struggles with this.

I know how they feel. I feel the same way every Sunday afternoon. I have three young women who come to my house to engage in a small discipleship group. We often discuss what we're learning from Scripture or a book we're reading together and how it relates to the gospel and our lives. But every Sunday afternoon, in the couple of hours before they arrive, I hear the same refrain in my head: "Who am I to disciple these girls? I haven't spent good time with the Lord at all this week. I snapped at my husband this morning and am irritated with one of my children for not sweeping the floor. I've got these girls showing up in 30 minutes to a dirty kitchen, and I haven't even read my chapter yet! Lord, I've got nothing!"

THE UNQUALIFIED DISCIPLE

How do I answer the women in my church, when I know exactly how they feel? When they express doubt about their qualifications, I'm tempted to say, "That's not true! You've got a great marriage and are raising some stellar kids. You're hospitable and easy to talk to. You'll be fine!"

Though my praise might convince them, that response won't do. It certainly doesn't help me on Sunday afternoons when I feel neither great nor hospitable. I've had to go to the Scriptures to search out the truth. What does God's Word have to say about how we feel?

To some degree, what we are feeling is true. We don't have anything, in ourselves, to give. We see in the Scriptures that our hearts are deceitful and desperately sick and even beyond our ability to understand them (Jer. 17:9). We also see that anything we call righteousness basically amounts to a bunch of dirty rags that are only fit for the fire (Is. 64:6). In fact, there is not one of us who can claim righteousness on our own (Ps. 14:3). Jesus tells us unequivocally, "apart from me, you can do nothing" (Jn. 15:5). So if we're trying to dredge up righteousness and truth from inside ourselves in order to give that away to others, it's true. We've got nothing.

GOD'S QUALIFICATIONS

I think Moses felt the same way. When God approached him in the wilderness and instructed him to go and speak to the most powerful man in the land, Moses must have lifted his eyebrow just as I've seen the women in my church do. He said to God, "Who am I that I should go to Pharaoh and bring the children of Israel out of Egypt?" (Exod. 3:11) Moses was wanted for murder and had been tending sheep for most of his adult life. I'm sure inside he was screaming, "Me?! I've got nothing!"

But God doesn't assure Moses of his qualifications as I'm tempted to do with these women. No, on the contrary, God assures Moses of *God's qualifications*. God answers Moses's question of "Who am I?" with a resounding "I AM." This is the response we need to hear.

When women raise their eyebrows and express doubt about discipleship, my job is not to convince them that they are equal to the task. My job is to convince them that *God is equal to the task.* "You're right," I need to reply, "You've got nothing. Neither do I. But God has everything."

We can't forget that we're branches. By ourselves, we will bear no fruit. Worse than that, we will die. But attached to the vine, we feed off the life of Jesus and become healthy, bushy branches, laden with fruit to nourish others. Attached to the vine, we have a lot to give.

Jesus says it this way, "By this my Father is glorified, that you bear much fruit and so prove to be my disciples" (Jn. 15:8). And as we bear fruit, we share that fruit and make more disciples, all the while bringing glory to the Father. You've got nothing, you say? Oh, no. If you're attached to the vine, you've got everything.

GOSPEL OPPORTUNITIES

The hesitancy that we feel when it comes to engaging in a discipleship relationship is real. We know ourselves better than anyone. We know our past mistakes and our current failings. We think that these disqualify us from leading anyone in discipleship, but actually the reverse is true. *Our very hesitations are gospel opportunities.*

When we remember that we're branches, we remember that what is flowing through the branch is the life of Jesus, the gospel itself. The gospel! The good news! The gospel reminds us that we don't have to live a perfect life in order to engage in discipleship. Jesus lived the perfect life in our place. He died to take the punishment for all our mistakes and failings. Then, praise God, he rose from the dead, canceling our debt and disarming the power of sin in our lives. This is what we give to others in discipleship: the good news of the gospel!

Sunday afternoons are going to look different at my house. When I look around at my dirty floor and my unread chapters, I am going to remind myself that I am not giving these girls myself, I am giving them Jesus. I am not attempting to present to them a perfect life, but Jesus's perfect life. My goal is not to show them how to do everything right, but to apply the gospel when we do everything wrong.

When I hear the familiar refrain, "I've got nothing!" I will reply with certainty, "If you've got the gospel, you've got everything."

31

BE FRUITFUL AND MULTIPLY
Seth McBee

Historically, movements have stopped because they were primarily leader-led information dumps. Information isn't a bad thing, but information-driven movements are limited in influence. Why can we create disciple multiplying movements?

IT'S WHAT WE WERE MADE FOR

In the Garden of Eden, we see that we as image-bearers of God were made to be fruitful and multiply (Gen. 1:22, 26-28). By issuing his first "great commission," God did not merely intend for us to have more people over for Thanksgiving dinner. Rather, he wanted his beautiful image to fill the entire earth through the multiplication of his image-bearers. But through Adam, we sinned and were separated from God.

In the attempt to author our own story, we sought center stage–pushing God's goals for us aside. We sought to multiply our image for the sake of our own fame rather than God's fame.

When someone repents and turns to God, it is our responsibility to show them their new mission by pointing back to the garden. We must show how their mission is all about multiplying for the sake of God's glory not multiplying a life that is all about them and their legacy.

Most small groups in churches believe their goal is to get to know each other or form a close bond. If this is the goal, multiplication will never be desired. Drawing close to one another is not the goal of missional community, but making disciples who make disciples is (being fruitful and multiplying images of

Jesus). Drawing close to one another happens because Jesus has given us the same Father, and we are a part of the same family. So, forming a close bond is a bi-product rather than the goal of living together on mission as family.

THIS MUST BE ON OUR LIPS

If our goal is to make disciples who make disciples (to be fruitful and multiply), then this must be on our lips constantly. I tell those who aren't even followers of Jesus yet that we desire to see communities like ours across the world doing the same thing. So, when they join our community as a follower of Jesus, they've already been discipled to know that we desire multiplication.

But it doesn't stop there. We continue to talk about it as a group and continue to seek to hear from the Spirit on his timing and his power to send us out. The best way I can describe this is by relating it to your child. Do you desire to see your child stay in your house until they die? Or do you desire to see them leave the house and have a family of their own? Do you then wait until they are 18 and spring this on them and then kick them out? Or, do you continue talking to them about it, train them and seek for them to be ready when the day comes to leave your house and go and be fruitful and multiply with their new family? This is the same thing we need to be doing with our church families. We need to seek to see them grow in maturity and grow in the gospel so that they too can lead a family of missionary servants to live out the effects of the gospel with those around them.

People often ask me how I make it easy for our groups to multiply. I give the same advice every time: you must regularly talk about multiplication and train the next group for its certainty. It must always be on your lips and prayers, and always on your people's lips and prayers. If it's not, then it will be very difficult when it happens–like kicking out your unsuspecting child and telling them it's healthy.

TRANSFORMING AND TRANSFERRABLE

You will do well by building the foundation of multiplication. You will also do well by regularly talking about it and listening to the Spirit in the process. But what happens if you have no leaders to lead the multiplication? This is where many groups and movements fail. The reason is that people in the group look at the leader and think, "There's no way I can do what he's doing. This takes too much time and too much theological knowledge." Not only that, but you've merely spoken about multiplication without transforming people's hearts to seek it out.

Merely talking about making disciples is sometimes fun and it's a great theological exercise for the mind. But mere talk and theologizing rarely inspire people to make disciples.

If you desire to see others gripped to make disciples, you must not only penetrate their intellect. You must also aim at their hearts. If you merely aim at their heads with theological reasons why it's good to make disciples, people will always come up with reasons why they are not convinced of its realities.

I think of Jonathan Edwards when he spoke of God's holiness and grace and compared it to honey.

In this way, he says, there is a difference between having an opinion that God is holy and gracious, and having a sense of the loveliness and beauty of that holiness and grace. There is a difference between having a rational judgment that honey is sweet, and having a sense of its sweetness. A man may have the former, that knows not how honey tastes; but a man cannot have the latter unless he has an idea of the taste of honey in his mind. So there is a difference between believing that a person is beautiful, and having a sense of his beauty. The former may be obtained by hearsay, but the latter only by seeing the countenance. When the heart is sensible of the beauty and amiableness of a thing, it necessarily feels pleasure in the apprehension. It is implied in a person's being heartily sensible of the loveliness of a thing, that the idea of it is sweet and pleasant to his soul; which is a far different thing from having a rational opinion that it is excellent.

As disciples, we must show others what it means to make disciples. When a follower of Jesus sees new disciples being made and they are a part of it, their heart will rejoice. And like honey on the lips, they will desire more honey instead of merely talking about honey. Jesus did the same with the blind man in John 9. He healed him so that the blind man would taste and see that the Lord was good. Then he supported that heart-transforming act, to theologically tackle the implications of who Jesus was afterward in John 9:35-41. Notice the way the blind man desired others to taste and see that the Lord Jesus was good–because his heart was transformed.

Not only do we seek to transform, but we must also make sure what we do is transferrable. I have many things I can share from experience that I believe are transferrable for my people, but you must ask yourself these types of questions:

- **Do I need a theological degree to lead the community like I do?** Remember, not all people like to read and study as much as many of us pastors do. If we want to create a movement of disciple-making, then we have to move away from leading from a position of "trained" men, into leading like "untrained" men. (By the way, I've never been to seminary, nor am I paid by the church.)

- **Do I need to be paid by the church to have the time to do what I do?** See above.

- **What resources are available to give future leaders so that they don't feel like they have to think of new topics to discuss and study in their Missional Community?** I do not do any book studies in the Bible that cause me to do an immeasurable amount of study and reading on my own. If I do, then people will see the group as one that can only be led by someone with my capacity. Instead, I use easily transferrable studies (e.g., www.bild.org)

- **How can I model all of this, so that I am going to be able to transfer leadership, instead of being the functional savior for our groups?** Make sure you lead as you want others to lead. Don't do studies that can only be led by a seminarian. Don't do so many activities that can only be done by those with a job inside the church. Remember, as you lead, you are discipling those in your group on what it looks like to lead a group of disciple-makers. You can't say one thing and model another. They'll see right through that.

Because I have worked hard to hear the Spirit's leading in this, 80% of those I lead desire to lead someone else. When I baptized a new disciple, he first desired to lead a group of disciple-makers. He saw this as the only option for someone who was a follower of Jesus and, that it wasn't anything special. In spite of being a new disciple, he didn't see this as some "high calling" only for a few.

Since we want to lay the foundation of multiplication, we regularly talk about making disciples who make disciples. We seek to do this by modeling it for them in ways easily transferrable. New disciples often can't wait to lead others in the making of disciples who multiply to make more disciples.

So, go! Be fruitful disciples of Jesus by multiplying his beautiful image everywhere.

32

LEADING JOE BLOW INTO MISSION
Seth McBee

All around the world, pastors and church leaders say the same thing. We need more leaders. We speak about these leaders as though God has sent us on a snipe hunt and is laughing at us as we search for these leaders in the bushes.

The fact is you have tons of leaders in your church family right now. The key is to lead your people in a way that effectively trains leaders who also train leaders.

I have an interesting perspective on this topic. I am both a preaching elder in our church and the owner of a business. To put it bluntly, I am busy. But don't let me fool you. I am not busier than anybody else. Almost every conversation I have around the coffee and donut table at church goes like this:

Me: *How have you been?*

The Entire Church (even the 9 year old playing tag): *Busy.*

It doesn't matter if you're speaking to an executive on Wall Street or an executive of the home (props to the stay at home mom), everybody's busy these days. But if you perceive yourself and others as busy, how can leaders ever emerge from your church to lead others on the mission? How can any disciples of Jesus ever be made? Let me suggest some things.

1. START WITH THE GOSPEL
I know this seems *very* Christian of me to say, but the fact is we, and the people we lead, need to be motivated by the *good news*, not motivated by what we do. God has given us a new identity,

changed us from enemies to his children. He did it all by his work, not our effort.

Not only has God done this in justification, but he does this in sanctification. When we are bearing fruit worthy of repentance, it is because it has been through his power and grace, not our merit and works.

I remember sitting under the preaching of Mike Gunn, Jeff Vanderstelt, and Caesar Kalinowski. I was getting "gospeled" each week. It was like God was taking their words and beating the moralism out of my heart. I was so compelled that this good news wasn't just for yesterday, but for today and tomorrow. My wife and I naturally asked, "How can we make sure everyone around us knows about THIS good news?"

When we hear truly good news, we want to share it and live in the light of it. If good news is phony, who cares? Meaning, if the gospel was good for us once upon a time (like when we walked down the aisle or raised our hand when everyone had their heads bowed and eyes half shut) but it isn't even better for us today, then that becomes a burden to carry, not a load that we've given to the Savior.

Everything you do as a leader/pastor has to start with the gospel motivation of who God is, what God has done, who we are, and what we need to do. When the gospel is correctly and authentically preached, shared, and lived out in community, people will naturally (by the new Spirit) desire to live it out.

2. HAVE REALISTIC GOALS FOR LEADERS

Imagine what you want a leader to look like in your church. I'm talking about everyone. The single mom, the single dad, the mentally handicapped, the disabled, the CEO, the college students, the children, everyone.

When thinking of leadership, most of us really have a narrow view. For whatever reason, we think a leader must be someone who can preach, know every dark corner of theology, take over Bible studies, and write a thesis on the Nephilim in Genesis.

Additionally, many pastors think every leader should be just like them. The problem with this thinking is:

- If you could raise leaders to be a replica of you, you'd be out of a job.
- Your people don't have time to be like you. That's why they pay you—to equip them for the point of all ministry.

So, what is realistic for leaders in your church? The answer is simple. They need to do exactly what God has called all of us to do: make disciples of Jesus who make more disciples of Jesus.

Jesus tells us, in short order that making disciples is done by his power and authority (Matt. 28; Acts 1:8). He tells us to do this with the term "go," which means more accurately "as you go." He tells us that we are his body, the parts of which have many different functions. Your people have been designed and formed by how God wants them to be. He has placed them in the place he desires. The power is not by their will but by God's might and wisdom.

Think of this. If you tell your people that the goal is to make disciples and to do this where they are right now, how much of a burden have you just released from their shoulders?

To tell the stay at home mom that she can't live two lives only one and to live this one life for the glory of God, then she can go to the mom's group and be a light to them. She can invite other moms over and have a play date and befriend them to show them and tell them about Jesus. She's probably already doing some of these things, but now she is released to do it in the power of the Spirit for the glory of God to make disciples.

Think of the burden released if you don't have programs in your church where everyone has to attend, but they live their life with the family of God to show off who God is where they are sent.

Instead of telling someone you need to show up for Vacation Bible School to teach for those five days from morning until night, you send them back to their neighborhoods and keep doing the things they do, but to do them with non-Christians and Christians, to fully-form disciples who then go and make more disciples.

Just ask your people to take an inventory of what they are doing now and have them start thinking how they can start doing those things with the power of the Spirit with the goal of living out the great commission.

All these things can be turned into times of disciple making. (Don't let this statement fool you, we are always making disciples. It's just a matter if we are making disciples of us or Jesus.):

- Coaching sport teams
- Work
- Going to the gym
- Neighborhood Parties
- Dinner at your house
- Hanging out in the front yard
- PTA
- Community Events

The list goes on and on.

3. SHARE MEALS

If you want an easy start, given to me by Caesar Kalinowski, tell your people this:

We eat 21 times per week. Each person eats 1 meal with a not-yet believer twice a month. That's 2 meals out of 84 meals. If a family has another family over that counts as 1 out of 4. Then come together and share about your conversations and start praying like crazy to know what the Spirit would have you do next with each person you've shared a meal with.

The simplicity of this, and the conversations that come from this will show your people what you mean by making disciples and doing it in the everyday.

The point is, when you release your people back to the areas that God has already place them in, then not only do you have job security as a pastor, but people see the importance of the work God has given them. Some may see what they're doing and adjust because of this simple calling, they might move to be more effective. So discuss what's happening with your leaders as they pursue discipleship wherever God places them.

Think of the power of this. You have stay at home moms, single moms, dads, working parents, college kids, CEOs, garbage men, teachers, politicians, web designers, and accountants all living out the power given to them by the Spirit to make disciples where God has sent them. Doesn't this sound like a fully functioning body that will show off the entirety of Jesus, instead of one small facet?

This is what it means to fill the earth with his glory. Every part of the earth is seeing Jesus because we empower our people, instead of treating them as though they have to be full time pastors to fulfill the job of making disciples.

Start simple. We are told that he who is entrusted with little can be trusted with much. Give them these simple ideas to live out and watch as God calls them to more and more.

Just as you wouldn't feed an infant steak, neither should we tell our people that to make disciples they must move to Africa in order to make disciples. Let God show them what they should do.

4. SHOW THEM HOW TO LEAD

You can talk about training leaders all day, but if you don't show people how to lead, they'll never fully grasp it. I believe that you as the pastor cannot do this alone. Know that the people who are not pastors—yet who are already living this out—are your best allies.

Think of this. Nearly every person in your church receives zero income from the church but are still called to make disciples. If this is true, you should be leading them from that perspective, but you also need folks who can lead by example. In other words, to paraphrase Jeff Vanderstelt, instead of saying 99% are not paid to make disciples, we should be saying that 100% of God's people are paid to make disciples. It's just a matter of where God directs that money from.

When you have a missional community meeting and you start going through a study, don't draw up some study from Leviticus that you created and spend the whole time preaching at the group. Who else is going to have time for that? What about those who hate speaking to groups? Lead your people in a way where they can say to themselves, "I can do that."

Look for material that is easily transferrable to everyone. If every time you have some sort of a study in your missional community you are the one writing up the questions and leading the study, how will anyone have time to do the same? Set them an example of what they can do. We just keep speaking and living in a way that demands that we learn with our heads, be motivated by the new heart given by the Spirit, and walk it out with our feet empowered by the Spirit.

Don't do it alone. Ever. Always be taking people with you or showing it to them as family. This way your people are not only hearing it from your lips, but experiencing it with their feet.

Your people will learn how to make disciples by the way *you* make disciples. If you only do it with deep studies in a formal setting, then they'll think they have to copy you. If you show them you can only make disciples by having BBQ's every Friday, then they'll think that the road to gospel living is paved by Weber grills. But, if you can show them that it happens in everyday life, in every facet of life, with all kinds of people, you'll show them the ways of Jesus.

Jesus wants everyone to make disciples, but we have set up our people for failure because we only want leaders who look like full time paid pastors or professional party throwers. (Both of those are awesome by the way.)

So, in the end, how do we find and develop leaders?

First, motivate people with the gospel. Making disciples doesn't gain your favor or acceptance from God, but is the natural fruit born of a child of God. Second, tell them that God has placed them where they are now, doing what they are doing now, to make disciples by his power. Third, show them what you mean by living your life in the way the other 99% of your people can succeed in making disciples. Finally, do all this by starting simply with small steps. And wait on God to reveal the next steps for everyone in your community.

33

7 WAYS TO KEEP YOUR MISSIONAL COMMUNITY FROM MULTIPLYING
Seth McBee

A missional community (MC) can be defined as a family of missionary servants who are sent to make disciples who make disciples. When trying to understand what a MC is, it may be best described as people living as a family. So, when one has a question about the function of a MC, most of the time the answer is found by asking, "How would a healthy family answer that question?" One of the major differences found in MCs vs. traditional small groups is this idea of multiplication, which is built in the very story of God from the beginning in the very first family.

In the Garden of Eden, we see that as image-bearers of God we were made to be fruitful and multiply (Gen. 1:22, 26-28). By issuing his first "great commission," God did not merely intend for us to have more people over for Thanksgiving dinner. Rather, he wanted his beautiful image to fill the entire earth through the multiplication of his image-bearers. But through Adam, we sinned and were separated from God.

In the attempt to author our own story, we sought center stage–pushing God's goals for aside for our own desires. We sought to multiply our image for the sake of our own fame rather than God's fame.

When someone repents and turns to God, it is our responsibility to show them their new mission by pointing back to the garden. We must show how their mission is all about multiplying for the sake of God's glory, not multiplying a life that is all about them and their legacy.

Many small groups in churches believe their goal is to get to know each other or form a close bond. This is not necessarily a bad thing. However, if this is the main goal, multiplication will never be desired. Drawing close to one another is not the primary goal of a MC; rather, making disciples who make disciples is the lifeblood of MC life. Disciples are fruitful and multiply disciples of Jesus. Drawing close to one another happens because Jesus has given us the same Father, and we are a part of the same family. So, forming a close bond is a bi-product rather than the primary goal of living together on mission as family.

If we take this idea of multiplication to how we see a healthy family, you can think of it in this way: A healthy family doesn't stay a close family unit forever, living in the same house with no expectations of the child leaving the house. We train them up, we teach them, and we disciple them so that when they reach a certain age they are then sent out to start their own life, their own family.

STUNTING MULTIPLICATION

In my years of planting and leading MCs, I've found that MCs struggle to multiply, or sometimes they don't want to multiply at all. Sometimes they aren't trained properly and don't know any better, and sometimes they would rather stay the same group of people year after year without adding anyone new. There are various other reasons why they may not multiply, but after talking with leaders, it's not long before I can understand why they aren't multiplying. In this article, we will look at some of the most popular mistakes I've seen that keep MCs stagnant.

Before we continue, please know this: I am not forgetting the work of the Spirit or the plans of God. Let's be honest, God has used a burning bush and a talking donkey, so if he wants something to happen, he'll make it so. Instead, I am writing this purely from a planning and strategic understanding of leading MCs. No one will multiply without God's Spirit empowering and leading that multiplication, but multiplication also takes hard work and intentional direction.

Here are some ways to ensure that your MC never multiplies. If you follow these simple steps, you'll ensure yourself a long life of hanging out with the same people, studying the same things, and never having to actually live them out or teach them to others.

1. NEVER ASK ANYONE TO STEP UP AND LEAD

One of the best ways to ensure that you don't multiply is to assume the role of end-all leader for your group. Make sure the buck always stops with you. The last thing you want to do is to try and empower anyone for leadership. They should never think that they could actually lead a community on mission someday. So, when you go to trainings, when you are thinking through the next steps for the MC, when you are living your life of discipleship during the week, never invite anyone from the group into your life. Who knows? They might learn from you, apply it on their own life, and get the idea that they could lead too.

2. DON'T HAVE A UNIFIED CONTEXT FOR MISSION

The mission is to make disciples, just make sure that your MC doesn't have a unified context of who you are trying to reach. Stay scattered. Have people do their own thing, then just come back and talk about how things are going. The last thing you want to see is everyone being unified for the sake of mission, because that will only lead to a ton of gospel conversations, tons of idols being exposed in each other's lives, and the church looking like a body to the outside world. The more unified you are in mission the more people that would attract, and that only leads to one thing: multiplication. Imagine if the world saw a group of people who gave up time, money, and comfort for the sake of a unified goal!

3. DO NOT HAVE A WRITTEN VISION AND PLAN TO MAKE DISCIPLES

Keep this all organic. No planning. You don't want this to look like an organization, or even worse, organized religion. I mean, isn't that how the Apostle Paul did things? He just got up, went out, and hoped for the best. If you have a written vision or plan, then there are expectations. Where there are expectations, people might feel like they need to get involved. If there is a plan, you have to actually think through your mission and hold each other accountable. If there is a plan, you can see the steps it's going to take to make disciples in a particular area. Not only this, but these plans give you specifics of how to pray to the Spirit on how he can accomplish this plan or open your eyes to the plan that he desires. Too much planning actually leads to too much dependence on the Spirit, and you wouldn't want to be one of "those churches."

4. DON'T INTERACT WITH UNBELIEVERS

Make sure you focus only on the "one anothers" in the New Testament. What does it matter if Jesus taught his disciples how to disciple in the midst of unbelievers? If you interact with unbelievers they get in the way. Unbelievers don't always believe what you believe, and you want people around you who believe like you so that everyone gets along smoothly. If you interact with unbelievers, they might revile you or hate you. What happens if an unbeliever actually watches your life and sees who the real Jesus is? What if they decide to follow him, too? That messes up your group dynamic that has been together for the last few years. Instead, just take care of each other and pray like crazy that Jesus returns as fast as possible.

5. KEEP IT AN EVENT INSTEAD OF A RHYTHM

If you can keep our MC looking like an event each week, then that will make sure that people see it as merely another type of small group. That way, you can just get together, have dinner, study the Bible, and then see each other again in another week. You don't need to advance the mission; they can just keep coming to your group instead. Plus, if you keep it an event, less people desire to have another meeting in their life or in their home. They will feel overwhelmed to plan everything around this event, and it will add stress to their lives. If you add stress to someone's life, you definitely will not get all those busy people desiring to multiply the group. Rhythms bring forth the idea of freedom and rest and fun, the idea that it's part of life rather than a meeting. This is a tempting idea that you don't want to convey to outsiders.

6. TEACH AT THE MEETINGS LIKE A PROFESSIONAL

One of the best ways to ensure that you don't multiply is to make sure you train and teach those in your MC in a way where they'll say, "I could never do that." So, write up your own Bible studies with quizzes, teach from the Greek Bible, and wow everyone with your expansive knowledge that rivals the Apostle Paul. The more you are able to do things in your MC that cannot be transferrable, the better. That way, everyone will know that there is no way they can emulate what their leader is doing. If they can't emulate, how will anyone multiply? Bingo. Never use material that someone could wrap their minds around or easily teach to others. Always reinvent the wheel and make sure your community understands that if they want to lead an MC, they must get more training than an astronaut.

7. DON'T TALK ABOUT MULTIPLICATION OR THE SPIRIT

One of the easiest ways to create an atmosphere of never multiplying is by simply never talking about it. Make sure people don't expect it. Healthy things multiply, and you don't want to give off that vibe. Talk about how great it is to have the same people in the MC for so long, and remind them that outsiders would mess up the chemistry. Who cares if you haven't impacted other people's lives, you've impacted the group and that should be enough! The person who is primarily responsible for multiplication is the Spirit, so make sure that he is left completely out of the conversation. Don't talk about him. He's dangerous. He has a ton of power and has done things you should only read about in Acts and not experience in your own life.

Disclaimer: Please know that this is purely fun and sarcastic. This is not meant to hurt anyone or to mock anyone. My real hope is that you'll see some things you can change or start working towards so that you can multiply your MCs for the sake of making disciples of Jesus.

34

10 WAYS TO KILL COMMUNITY
J. A. Medders

I don't mean to be an alarmist, but there are some flinching verses in the New Testament when it comes to the necessity of being in Christian community. Being "in Christ," being a Christian, means that we are with Christ's people. A gospel-centered life will always involve the company of the gospel, the redeemed saints of God. A life that is worthy of the gospel will bob in the wake of a gospel community.

> Only let your manner of life be worthy of the gospel of Christ, so that whether I come and see you or am absent, I may hear of you that you are standing firm in one spirit, with one mind striving side by side for the faith of the gospel. (Phil. 1:27)

According to Paul, a life that is in step with the gospel is a life in sync with the Christian community, being gospel-focused together. If we are serious about the gospel, we will be serious about community. There are ten community killers that we must avoid. One from Hebrews 10 and nine more from Colossians 3.

10. DON'T MEET WITH OTHER CHRISTIANS

"And let us consider how to stir up one another to love and good works, not neglecting to meet together, as is the habit of

some, but encouraging one another, and all the more
as you see the Day drawing near" (Heb. 10:24–25).

The author of Hebrews couldn't have been clearer: "Don't
neglect meeting together." The Christian life is a community
life. It's with the Church. To truly walk with Jesus is to walk
with Jesus's people. Consider the New Testament books. Every
New Testament letter, except four (1–2 Timothy, Titus, and
Philemon), are written to churches. We can't obey the New Testament, or practically understand its context, without the community. We are to live in community not just for ourselves, but
also for one another. To stir up others and have them stir us to
love Jesus and spread the fame of his name. Our American de-
fault is, "What will I get out of this?" Here's the answer: What
you get is loving and serving others.

Community is so essential; I think eternity depends on it.
Hebrews 10:24–25 is one of the classic community passages—and for good reason. But have you notice the eschato-
logical impetus in the text? "And let us consider how to stir up
one another to love and good works, not neglecting to meet together, as is the habit of some, but encouraging one another,
and *all the more as you see the Day drawing near*" (Heb. 10:24–
25). There are two important questions two dwell on. Who are
the 'some'? And why talk about the 'Day'?

Who are the "some"? It's those who have made a habit of
not meeting and being with other Christians. Two groups of
Christians in the verse: Christians that meet together; Christians
that don't meet together. This is a warning in Hebrews. Eventually, it's those who have abandoned the Church, distanced
themselves from community, and therefore they have abandoned Christ. "They went out from us, but they were not of us;
for if they had been of us, they would have continued with us.
But they went out, that it might become plain that they all are
not of us" (1 Jn. 2:19). Unbelievers, goats in sheep's clothing,
eventually stop grazing among the people of God.

Why talk about the Day? In a stellar passage about encouraging one another, why address the Day of the Lord, judgment,

and wrath? The writer of Hebrews also does this earlier in his letter:

> Take care, brothers, lest there be in any of you an evil, unbelieving heart, leading you to fall away from the living God. But exhort one another every day, as long as it is called 'today,' that none of you may be hardened by the deceitfulness of sin. For we have come to share in Christ, if indeed we hold our original confidence firm to the end. (Heb. 3:12–14)

He warns about falling away and holding fast till the end— which can be curtailed by the communal command "exhort one another."

The writer of Hebrews is saying, "Commune together, encourage each other, so you don't fall away." What about once saved always saved? Yes, amen. The Spirit seals all of those who are truly in Christ.

But the Bible says nothing about, "Once professed always protected." Profession, in a sense, is proven, revealed in obedience to Christ, the fruit of regeneration, "holding till the end." We are here to help each other stay the course for that Last Day. Community isn't just to help you get through the week—it's to get you through Judgment Day.

9. LIE ABOUT YOURSELF

"Do not lie to one another, seeing that you have put off the old self with its practices and have put on the new self, which is being renewed in knowledge after the image of its creator" (Col. 3:9–10).

Community thrives on honesty, light, and love. Paul urges us not to lie to one another because he knows we will be tempted to hide the truth about *how* we are doing and *what* we are doing. But remember, we have a new identity in Christ. We aren't our sins—we are Christ's. Once we believe that everyone one of us is in being renewed, and none have "arrived," the motivation to lie to will fly away.

8. FOCUS ON DIFFERENCES

"Here there is not Greek and Jew, circumcised and uncircumcised, barbarian, Scythian, slave, free; but Christ is all, and in all" (Col. 3:11).

Community isn't conformity. Unity isn't uniformity. We are all very different people. A lot of men in my church are obsessed with killing animals. I love eating animals. I've gone hunting with them; it was a lot of getting up early to see a whole lot of nothing. But do differences in hobbies mean we can't have community together? Do we have anything in common? You better believe we do: Christ. We are all different members of the body of Christ. Some are hands, feet, toes. You think the feet are interested in gloves? Think the hands are into shoes? No! But they know they need each other. Don't major on the minor differences. Christ is all, not us, at all.

7. HAVE A PRICKLY HEART

"Put on then, as God's chosen ones, holy and beloved, compassionate hearts, kindness, humility, meekness, and patience" (Col. 3:12).

It's one thing to show up to someone's house, and a horrible thing to be a cactus while you are there. Are you compassionate toward others or crusty? Gospel-centered people aren't allowed to be cranky people. It's out of step with the gospel of joy. "Jerks for Jesus" shouldn't be a thing, and sadly, that is how many Christians live. Peer into the gospel, and let it clothe you in the composure of Jesus of Nazareth.

6. DON'T BEAR WITH OTHERS

"Bearing with one another" (Col. 3:13).

Bearing with one another isn't, "Yes, they are ridiculous. I'll be the bigger person." Rather, it sounds like, "I love this person and I want to serve them like Christ has served me. I can do more than put up with them, I'll endure with them, and carry their burdens with them." Jesus calls us his friends, he laid his life down for us, he loves us, and now we lay our lives down for each other—because we love each other (Jn. 15:12–13). Selfishness won't do this.

5. DON'T FORGIVE

"If one has a complaint against another, forgiving each other; as the Lord has forgiven you, so you also must forgive" (Col. 3:13).

When we are living in gospel mode, we will be quick to forgive because the bloody cross is always in our sight. Christians aren't allowed to hold a grudge—that is anti-gospel. Forgive others from that soil outside of Jerusalem, muddled with the blood of Jesus, remembering that God has no grudge with you—therefore, we must forgive.

4. BE UNLOVING

"And above all these put on love, which binds everything together in perfect harmony" (Col. 3:14).

The gospel is love in action. "For God so loved, he gave." Love is more than a sentiment; it's always a sacrifice. Gospel-laden community will be filled with the brand of love spelled out by Paul: "Love is patient and kind; love does not envy or boast; it is not arrogant or rude. It does not insist on its own way; it is not irritable or resentful; it does not rejoice at wrongdoing, but rejoices with the truth. Love bears all things, believes all things, hopes all things, endures all things" (1 Cor. 13:4–7).

3. BE THANKLESS

"And let the peace of Christ rule in your hearts, to which indeed you were called in one body. And be thankful" (Col. 3:15).

If you don't have a disposition of thanks for the body of Christ, indifference isn't far away. Distance is around the corner. Community isn't a hamper on your schedule, it's a helper. Community isn't the gospel, but it is one of the gospel's multitudinous and glorious gifts of grace.

2. DON'T CARE ABOUT THE GROWTH OF OTHERS

"Let the word of Christ dwell in you richly, teaching and admonishing one another in all wisdom, singing psalms and hymns and spiritual songs, with thankfulness in your hearts to God" (Col. 3:16).

Our spiritual growth isn't just for us, it's for the community. Community is for the wellbeing of everyone, not just one—not just *you*. Christian community isn't just about doing some Bible study; it's coming together to say, "I want to help you grow. I want to be a part of developing the best you possible. Jesus is calling me to you. And I need you to do that for me, too."

1. DON'T LET CHRIST BE YOUR ALL

"And whatever you do, in word or deed, do everything in the name of the Lord Jesus, giving thanks to God the Father through him" (Col. 3:17).

If your life is all about Jesus, you will be about the things that Jesus is about—and Jesus is about his Church. Always and forever. When Jesus is our all, we will want to give our lives for the people that Jesus gave up his life for, his redeemed people. Holding back our lives from people in the church is one of the most anti-Christ things we could do. Rather, in word or deed, couch or coffee, potluck or grill out, prayer list or accountability time, let it all be done in the name of the Lord Jesus.

35

STEREOTYPES PREVENT LASTING COMMUNITY

Brent Thomas

In 2004, Pixar introduced *The Incredibles*, a family of superheroes posing as a "normal" suburban family. After a series of unfortunate incidents followed by equally unfortunate lawsuits, superheroes are forced into "the Superhero Relocation Program," in which they are forced to pose as normal citizens in order to evade any further legal action. Mr. Incredible and Elastigirl become Bob and Helen Parr, insurance agent and stay-at-home Mom, complete with three children.

As a result of their hidden superpowers, Bob and Helen's children are caught in a net of confusion. They know they are different but every voice they hear seems to say, "different is not good." Things come to a head when at dinner one night when their daughter, Violet, complains to her Mom, Helen: "We act normal, Mom! I want to be normal!" Their son, Dash, wrestles with similar issues. After being told he can't try out for the track team because he's too fast, Dash says: "But Dad always said our powers were nothing to be ashamed of, our powers make us special." His Mom responds by telling him that "everyone's special, Dash," to which he retorts: "Which is another way of saying no one is."

Though born different (with super powers), society no longer values their differences. Instead, they want the "supers," as they're known, to simply blend in and be like everyone else. Soon, Syndrome, a super villain, emerges wreaking havoc and giving the Supers no choice but to come out of retirement and use their powers to save the very people who want them to just be normal. They're not normal. It's only when they're are able to truly be themselves that they can rise to their full potential and fight the evil that threatens their world.

The movie raises interesting questions about perception versus identity. When urging the children to use their special powers, Helen gives them masks, saying: "Your identity is your most valuable possession. Protect it." At a climactic moment, Syndrome reveals plans to sell super weapons to everyone, noting that, "When everyone's super, no one will be." When we all fit the expectations, there's nothing left to differentiate us.

STEREOTYPES PREVENT REAL AND LASTING COMMUNITY

Sadly, this is exactly what much of what passes for Christian community does. We forget that each one of us is fearfully and wonderfully made. We expect everyone to look and act the same. Our community is weakened because we try to smooth out people's rough edges. We forget that our community is strongest when we encourage individuality, not at the expense of, but for the sake of community. Christians, of all people, should get this.

Near the middle of my time in seminary, John Piper preached in chapel. I don't remember most of the sermon, but I do remember that, at one point, he took an aside, mentioning that he was preaching to a room full of men who were training to do the same. He noted that when we graduated, most of us would try to emulate our favorite preachers, but we wouldn't be any good at it. Instead, he offered, "we should strive to become sanctified versions of ourselves rather than watered-down versions of someone else." That phrase has haunted me, in a good way, like no other during my subsequent years of following Jesus.

I have spent a good deal of my life in "ministry" being compared to and contrasted to celebrities and stereotypes. Everyone has their idea of whom and what a pastor should be. But it goes deeper. Everyone has their own idea of what a Christian should be. And when everyone has their own idea of what a Christian should look like, we race towards the middle: the blandest version possible (so as to not offend anyone, of course). The very people who should be the most distinct, expressing the most individuality for the sake of community, end up being watered down versions of a stereotyped celebrity that doesn't even exist: an idealized Christian who no one really likes and no one can actually be but everyone seems to think is the standard.

Western Christians have produced some of the most anemic community known to man. We have perpetuated closed-off, private, judgmental, and stereotypical environments where everyone feels an unspoken (or sometimes spoken) expectation that everyone should look and act the same. The result, of course is that what passes for community in many churches is nothing of the sort. People are afraid to let their idiosyncrasies show and many are afraid to be honest about their shortcomings and struggles because all the other Christians have it together (even though, of course, they really don't).

WHO WE REALLY ARE

Christians ought to be the most comfortable with who we are and the most welcoming and celebratory of uniqueness. We know we are "fearfully and wonderfully made" by God himself (Ps. 139:14). Though we were by nature children of wrath (Eph. 2:3) and enemies of God (Rom. 5:10), he has adopted us into his family (Rom. 8:15; Gal. 4:5; Eph. 1:5). We, who were once far from God, have been brought near to him (Eph. 2:13). We have become his children, his heirs (Rom. 8:17, Gal. 3:29, etc.). What is true of the Savior is becoming true of his people. He stands on our behalf even now interceding with his righteousness (Rom. 8:34). The Holy Spirit who raised Christ from the dead dwells in us (Rom. 8:11)!

There is a direct correlation between individuality and community. Community is strongest when people are most encouraged to explore their individuality; to just be themselves and walk in honesty. If we are free of needing people's approval, we are free to serve sacrificially.

WHY DOESN'T THIS HAPPEN?

Why do we allow stereotypes to typecast us into versions of likable but not real characters? Everyone knows the answer but no one likes it. We judge each other and hogtie real community because, deep down, we believe that it matters how you look before others and before God because that's how he loves us more! So, I become tied to your approval of a fake version of myself which means that I can never actually give myself up to truly serve you because I've created a weird co-dependency thing that you may or may not be aware of.

In short, we choose to believe lies. Jesus told us that the "Truth will set us free" (Jn. 8:32). If Truth sets us free, then it would seem that lies hold us captive. Deep down, we don't believe that God's acceptance of us is enough. We may not even be sure if it's sincere. So we are never free to truly be ourselves because it's always tied to a search for acceptance. But what if this is not the way God meant it to be?

HOW DOES GOD SEE YOU?

If you were to picture God looking down on you and your life, how do you picture his facial expression? What do you think he might say over your life? Would he say, *"Dang it, I've given Brent so many chances, why can't he just get it together?"* or, *"Oh man, I've just had it with Brent's failures! This has gotten ridiculous!"* What do you really think he would say of you and your life?

Do you remember when Jesus went out to his crazy cousin John to be baptized in the Jordan? Mark 1:10-11 tells us that when Jesus came up out of the water, the Spirit descended upon him in the form of a dove and a voice came from heaven saying, "You are my beloved Son; with you I am well pleased." What might change in our communities if individuals believed that what the Father says of the Son, he says about us? Because Jesus stands on our behalf, the Father loves us, he is pleased with us, and we do not have to work for his approval or anyone else's.

I wonder why our first thought is so rarely that God is pleased with us for who we are and not what we do? I have seven sons and one daughter (four biological sons, three foster sons and a foster daughter) and I love them each for who they are. They are each very different from each other. It would be foolish of me to expect them all to have the same interests, play the same sports, read the same books, listen to the same music, etc. It would be even more foolish if I based my acceptance of them on how well they all tried to act the same. And yet that's exactly what we often do to one another.

THE FRUIT OF DISBELIEF

We don't believe that God truly loves us for who we are so we don't believe that anyone else will love us for who we are. We pretend and there's no real community because no one is really themselves because everyone has adopted a false caricature of what we should all look like. Since our relationships are bound up in seeking approval, we never have the freedom to truly serve one another.

But the Truth sets us free. What if I no longer need your approval because I have God's approval through Jesus? Now, I am free to be myself which enables me to serve you sacrificially because I no longer need your approval. It doesn't matter what you think of me. I can and will find ways to show you God's love. Because I can, not because I should.

When Jesus sets us free to truly be ourselves, community flourishes. And as community flourishes, I am even more comfortable showing you just how screwed up I am. And community flourishes as we accept one another as a "beautiful circus of crazies and freaks" to quote my friend Aaron Spiro. But we won't ever have real community until we accept one another for who we are because we've accepted ourselves for who God has made us to be. And only the gospel can do that.

36

THE IDOL OF HOSPITALITY
Danielle Brooks

My husband and I host people in our home all the time. We are called to live in community with one another. We strive to live in community on a regular basis, but with that community comes hosting duties. As a hostess I provide food, entertainment, and above all make sure my house is clean. These three things can become an obsession for me, so much in fact that I find I never leave the kitchen. It's unbelievably easy to get wrapped up in the details and not enjoy our company. We get so distracted with preparing that we leave little time for fellowship and gospel-intentionality.

When I get so consumed with preparing, the story of Mary and Martha hits home for me.

HOSPITALITY: GIFT OR IDOL?

While Jesus is traveling, Martha opens her home to him. At this point, Jesus is pretty popular in some circles. He isn't just traveling with the 12 anymore. There are crowds following him. I picture Martha's house resembling a sardine can, so I see why Martha felt the need to get everything ready.

Can we all relate to Martha? Don't we all get a little apprehensive about having people over? Will there be enough food? Is my house clean enough? This concern and attention to detail can spread into a much bigger problem. Hospitality is a spiritual gift, but it can quickly become an idol.

I can't count how many times I have been cleaning in the kitchen alone when people are over. People leave their plates everywhere; someone needs to clean it up. It's my house so it's my responsibility. There is a mental checklist of things I have to get done before I can join everyone. The countertops are dirty, there are dishes in the sink, and the chip bowl is empty.

Like Martha, I am distracted by all of the service..

I get so encumbered by these tasks that I don't enjoy our company. My guests aren't here to watch me keep my house clean. They are here to fellowship with me, just like Jesus is there to fellowship with Mary and Martha. What can start as a little preparation can become a big distraction.

Mary gets it. She probably laid out some cheese and crackers and made it a point to get a good seat. So good a seat that she was literally "at his feet." Mary seems to be excited by the opportunity to spend time with Jesus. . Not only was Mary at Jesus's feet, but she also "listened to his teaching."

Meanwhile, Luke writes, Martha "was distracted with *much* serving."

This simple juxtaposition calls the posture of their hearts into question. While Martha's serving is not a bad thing, she quickly becomes consumed by it. Her heart is more centered on the hustle and bustle of having people over. Mary is captivated by Jesus. He is all she needs. Mary has centered her heart on Jesus.

Hebrews 12 says, "Let us lay aside every weight, and the sin which so easily ensnares us, and let us run with endurance the race that is set before us, looking to Jesus, the author and finisher of our faith..." Mary was laying aside every hindrance. She was intentional with her attention. I'm sure Mary knew there would be plenty of distractions, and she knew this was not the time to get caught up in them. Her sister, however, did not have the same perspective.

The Greek word for "serving" is *diakonian*, which means "ministry." Oh, how this changes my mindset when I read it as, "Martha was distracted with her *ministry*." How many times do we get caught up in our ministry we forget who we're doing it for? We are so distracted by the ministry itself we forget to focus our hearts on the one our ministry is for. Instead of looking up, we begin to selfishly look inward.

A CHANGE OF HEART

We worship a God who is jealous for our attention and we live in a world that offers an endless supply of distractions. I justify my behavior by saying, "Jesus, I'm doing this for you!" I need to clean up while people are here so there are no distractions between them and God. Jesus gently replies, "No my child, you are doing it for yourself, in my name. You are the distraction." Ouch.

Jesus replies the same way to Martha. The Message says, "Martha, dear Martha, you're fussing far too much and getting yourself worked up over nothing. One thing only is essential, and Mary has chosen it—it's the main course, and won't be taken from her."

Jesus isn't telling Martha that her preparations are bad. He is saying that they have taken his place in her heart. Only one thing is needed: a heart held captive by God. Mary has chosen what is essential.

I'm a Martha. I am anxious and troubled about a huge list of things that have to get done before I can sit down. We have people over to eat good food and enjoy one another's company. I want my home to be a welcoming hospital for the broken and hurting of the world to come in and be healed by the Physician. But the Spirit cannot speak through me when I am distracted with the ministry of "doing". Christ no longer holds my heart captive, my selfish desires do.

My friend recently took her daughter to story time at the library. The children were seated looking at the storyteller. Every child had a view of the book until her child decided to stand up for a better view. She blocked everyone else's view of the book. The other kids were now focused on her and not the story. They couldn't see through her to the storyteller.

Martha was so consumed with her ministry she blocks the view of Jesus. "She went up to him and said, 'Lord, do you not care that my sister has left me to serve alone? Tell her then to help me.'" (Lk. 10:40) How often are we the ones who stand up in front of Jesus while blocking others' view? And we do it in the name of our ministry.

CHRIST-CENTERED GATHERINGS

So how do we stay Christ-centered at a simple gathering? For me, it means putting 2 Corinthians 10:5 into practice by "taking captive every thought to make it obedient to Christ." When I get the itch to do the dishes that are piling up, I say a quick prayer to refocus my heart on Christ. Through the gospel, he alone offers me freedom from idolizing hospitality toward others.

It's okay to be prepared, but as soon as the door opens, preparation should stop. Chances are, your house is already spotless and most of the food is ready to go. You've been there, done that. Something will always need to be cleaned, but company will not always be with you. So when you feel a Martha tendency surfacing, refocus your heart. Make Christ the 'main course' of your fellowship because it can't be taken from you. Your friends are willingly walking into a Christ-centered environment, so make the most of it for Christ and the gospel.

In the grand scheme of things, what will you remember later in life? Will you remember you checked everything off your to-do list? Or how awesome it was to experience God's presence in your home? Let's make it a priority to focus on Christ who is Lord of our ministries rather than the ministry itself.

37

BRINGING THE MULTIPLICATION MINDSET HOME
Joey Cochran

Long days are draining. You need rest, but you're not actually expecting it. You're preparing yourself for children's excited voices greeting you. You're ramping up to mediate disputes between them, hopefully about who gets to hug you first. You also might greet a relieved spouse, fatigued from a long day of either being with the children or being at a long day of work.

You'd think the daily re-assimilation into home would be seamless. But it isn't, is it? Sometimes we are not spiritually or mentally prepared for it. Sometimes we are exhausted and our guard is down against pride and selfishness, resulting in ruinous family patterns.

Knowing this, practicing a routine that prepares the heart, soul, and mind for re-assimilation into family life is essential. It is an intentional discipline not just for your spiritual formation, but also for your wife's and your children's. It's a small step taken as you lead and disciple them. In turn, you and they will duplicate the mindset in all other discipleship environments: school, work, extra-curricular environments, and third places. When we approach every place with this mindset, we are better prepared disciple multipliers.

Obviously, the mindset shift into a new environment is not always successfully executed. This is the case particularly for fathers or mothers re-entering home environments after a long day of work. That's why I picked this one to discuss. It's easy to re-engage home with work-brain. But when we shift to home-brain, much discipleship fruit is cultivated. And so is the model for your children to duplicate as they multiply disciples in other contexts (2 Tim. 2:2).

It takes only a few minutes each day to prepare our mindset. We can do this in our car before departing from work, or as we are driving home, or sitting in the driveway. It's a really simple and classic process: shift your mindset, read Scripture, and pray.

1. SHIFT YOUR MINDSET

Shifting our mindset is not some rote process. It is an intentional plan of engagement where we earnestly decide that what is ahead is more important than what is left behind. Thus, we plan to lay aside our pocket screens, ignore notifications, and push back any residual work until after little ones are tucked in bed. This is also when we place work cares upon Christ; anger, fear, anxiety are relinquished in him (1 Pt. 5:7).

We prepare our minds for inquiry. We want to be quizzical of how the day went: the joys, trials, conflicts, surprises—all that took place during our absence. And quite honestly, a stay-at-home spouse will crave adult conversation, so we must be prepared to listen.

We also want to enter with the posture of service. Typically, I am in the practice of swooping into the home and whisking all three children away for a walk or playtime at the community playground while my wife, who is the one staying at home in our case, gets 15-30 minutes of quiet solitude.

Most working dads—if they are honest—have a Ward Cleaver or George Banks expectation for home arrival: immaculate home, hot dinner, spotless and perfectly behaved tykes, and wife in a dress and pearls. My mindset is a little different. I'm hoping for no fire, flood, or other acts of God to have occurred. But most of the time, I'm certain a tornado hit our kid's room.

However, we should have realistic expectations rather than idealistic expectations. God, fully anticipating our fallen condition, has been long in suffering with all our short failings. We, likewise, should follow in his step, not expecting a picture of Eden when we arrive home.

2. READ SCRIPTURE

Thomas Watson said, "The Scripture is the compass by which the rudder of our will is to be steered." My will is prone to drift off a God-glorifying course due to the desires of my flesh. Scripture is what holds the course of the mindset.

It's not enough to think on Scripture; we must share Scripture, too. We should be primary feeders of Scripture to our children. What if we had a Scripture to share with our children every time we returned home from work? How glorious would that be for our family? Not only would our will be set on the right course, but it sets a pattern for our children to be set on the right course with the right instrument to aid them: Scripture. When our mindset is built off Scripture, then it will be that much easier to mold our children's minds towards the same end. In many ways, this will be effectively caught more than taught, as long as we are contagiously and earnestly conversant with our children about what the Lord is teaching us.

In *Taking God at His Word*, Kevin DeYoung says, "The word of God is more than enough for the people of God to live their lives to the glory of God" (55). He's not just talking about Scripture's sufficiency to tackle the tough question of apologetics, theology, and our wrestling with doubt. DeYoung is saying Scripture is sufficient for everyday people to live everyday lives to the glory of an extraordinary God. Scripture dishes up helpings of truths that sufficiently ground us in the fruit of the Spirit and armor us to wage war against our enemy.

Thus, we're prepared to enter the foray of a potentially chaotic household. God's Word serves as a sufficient implement of peace in our hearts and homes. That peace is the peace of Christ. For Ephesians 2:17 says, "And he came and preached peace to you who were far off and peace to those who were near." That peace will then be spread afar by those whom we are training in our household to bear that peace to others. They will see us bring it, and they will long to share it with others.

3. PRAY

You will regret watching too much TV, playing too much Candy Crush, and reading too many tweets. You will never regret praying too much. You can't pray enough. Prayer is this incomprehensibly extraordinary gift where we have direct and full access to the God of the cosmos. He instructs us to ask for wisdom (Jas. 1:5) and to petition him with our requests (Phil. 4:6). Yet, we treat prayer like someone who picks a particular mobile carrier with unlimited talk minutes with a particular person, but who never actually called that person. That's precisely what we have—full access; and that's precisely what we do—full neglect.

Prayer doesn't produce a desired outcome as much as it transforms our current outlook. When we earnestly pray for our family before arriving home, it reorients our family around God rather than our children or ourselves. Helplessly bringing every concern, fear, or potential conflict to the Lord sets us up for entire dependence upon him for resolution. So often we rack our brains on how we can provide solutions and fix problems. Perhaps those tensions or problems exist not to give us something to troubleshoot, but to direct us to shoot the message of our troubles up to heaven. They become a grappling hook that draws us up to God.

If we're always praying about how we want things to change in our family, then it might just be us that require change. If nothing else, we need to open our eyes to the gift our spouse and children already are. They are a gift to steward, so we should ask God to show us how to steward, lead, and equip this gift as we prepare to commission them for gospel ministry.

So we shouldn't just deliver requests to God, we should express thanks and praise to him for our family as well. Before you head home is a great time to do this. It will—just like reading Scripture—facilitate that right mindset you wish to have when you return home each day.

I know what Scripture says about praying in our closet, but there is something valuable about praising God's answer to prayers before our spouse and children. If they never know that we've been praying for them, they will never have appreciation for God's answered prayer. They will also not share the same value and import prayer into their mission contexts. So don't just secretly pray for your family, openly discuss what you pray. Not only this, but solicit their prayer needs. That way, you can pray specifically for them as you are about to re-engage in your family context.

MULTIPLICATION IN MIND

Our society is programmed to pull families further and further apart over time. This is not healthy; it is actually potentially harmful. The more families are apart, the more false doctrine and false teachers may slyly slink into the family and corrupt convictions. This could slay souls.

Those few hours that exist after work and before bedtime are critical. They are the hours that we have to build into our family the stronghold of a Christian worldview. We're not just constructing a stronghold; we are training emissaries of our King. Our family will be sent out to herald good news to others. This means they must have first heard it from us, seen it demonstrated by us, tasted the fruit of it, and felt a stirring to multiply the process. Ones who have tasted the nectar of the gospel will naturally share it on to others.

CONTRIBUTORS

Brandon D. Smith is Executive Director of Gospel-Centered Discipleship and serves in editorial roles for *The Criswell Theological Review* and The Council on Biblical Manhood & Womanhood. He holds a B.A. in Biblical Studies from Dallas Baptist University, an M.A. in Systematic/Historical Theology from Criswell College, and will begin a Ph.D. in Systematic Theology at University of Aberdeen in 2015. He is proud to be Christa's husband and Harper Grace's daddy.

David Mathis is Executive Editor of DesiringGod.org and an elder at Bethlehem Baptist Church, Minneapolis. He has edited several books, including *Thinking. Loving. Doing.*, *Finish the Mission*, and *Acting the Miracle*, and is co-author of *How to Stay Christian in Seminary*.

Jonathan Parnell is a writer and content strategist at desiringGod.org. He lives in the Twin Cities with his wife, Melissa, and their four children, and is the co-author of *How to Stay Christian in Seminary*.

Tony Merida is a husband and father and the founding pastor of Imago Dei Church in Raleigh, NC. He also serves as a professor at Southeastern Baptist Theological Seminary, where he teaches church planting and preaching. His books include *Faithful Preaching*; *Ordinary*; *Orphanology* (co-author), and *Proclaiming Jesus* (GCD Books), and eight volumes (some forthcoming) in the new *Christ-Centered Exposition* commentary series (B&H), of which he also serves as a general editor, along with Danny Akin and David Platt.

Jeff Vanderstelt is the Visionary Leader of the Soma Family of Churches. He also serves as one of the teachers and elders of Soma Tacoma. Jeff has a passion to see the Church equipped and released to live on Jesus's mission through gospel intentionality in all of life. He lives in Tacoma, WA with his wife, Jayne, and their three kids.

Matt Brown is an evangelist, author of the upcoming book *Awakening: Why the Next Great Move of God is Right Under Our Nose* (Leafwood Publishers, 2015), and founder of Think Eternity. He and his wife Michelle are impacting thousands of people with the gospel each year through live events and online. They also minister to more than a quarter million followers on social media on a daily basis.

Jeremy Writebol is the Community Pastor at Journey the Way in Wichita, KS as well as Director of Porterbrook Kansas. He is the author of *everPresent: How the Gospel Relocates Us in the Present* (GCD Books) and several other articles at Gospel-Centered Discipleship. He is a graduate of Moody Bible Institute (B.A.) and The Resurgence Training Center (Missional Leadership). He and his wife Stephanie have two children.

Logan Gentry is Executive Pastor of Apostles Church in New York City. He blogs at Gentrified, is a regular contributor at Gospel-Centered Discipleship, and has contributed to The Gospel Coalition. Logan is married to Amber and they have three children.

Gib Gibson is married to Christina and lives in Columbia, SC. He is interested in church planting, the arts, and writing.

Alvin L. Reid is Professor Evangelism and Student Ministry and the Bailey Smith Chair of Evangelism at Southeastern Baptist Theological Seminary. A prolific author and popular speaker on topics including spiritual awakening, evangelism, missional Christianity, and the next generation, Alvin and his wife have lived in Wake Forest, NC for almost 20 years. They have two married children.

Stuart McCormack has ministered in a variety of churches and organizations in the U.K. and Thailand, making and maturing followers of Jesus. He has a B.A. in Theology and is currently studying for a Master's in Leading Innovation and Change. Stuart's day job involves coaching and supporting young people with life issues.

Luma Simms is a wife, mother, and writer, and author of *Gospel Amnesia: Forgetting the Goodness of the News* (GCD Books) and *Counterfeit Me* (Christian Focus, 2015).

Seth McBee is the adopted son of God, husband of one wife, and father of three. He's a graduate of Seattle Pacific University with a finance degree. By trade. Seth is President of McBee Advisors, Inc. He is also executive team member of the GCM Collective. He is the artist and co-author of the (free!) eBook, *Be The Church: Discipleship & Mission Made Simple.*

Nick Abraham holds an M.Div. from Liberty Baptist Theological Seminary. He lives in Navarre, OH with his wife and daughter. He currently serves as a Pastoral Intern at Alpine Bible Church in Sugarcreek, OH and works full-time at Smuckers.

Jonathan K. Dodson (MDiv; ThM, Gordon-Conwell Theological Seminary) serves as a pastor of City Life Church in Austin, Texas. He has written articles in numerous blogs and journals such as The Resurgence, The Journal of Biblical Counseling, and Boundless. He is author of *Gospel-Centered Discipleship, Raised?*, and *The Unbelievable Gospel* (Zondervan, 2014).

Dustin Crowe is the Local Outreach Coordinator at College Park Church in Indianapolis. He is pursuing an M.A. at Trinity Evangelical Divinity School and earned a B.A. in Historical Theology from the Moody Bible Institute. Dustin and his wife have been married for almost two years and still enjoy the no-kids stage.

Jeremy Carr is lead teaching pastor and co-founding elder of Redemption Church, an Acts 29 church in Augusta, GA. He is author of the book *Sound Words: Listening to the Scriptures* (GCD Books) and has written for the Resurgence. He holds an M.Div. and Th.M. Jeremy is husband to Melody and father to Emaline, Jude, Sadie, and Nora.

Jake Ledet is married to Ginger and daddy to Sophia, Wyatt, and Lily. He is a pastor at CityView Church, and he and Ginger lead Keller Covenant Counseling.

Brad Watson serves as a pastor at Bread & Wine Communities in Portland, OR. He lives in inner Southeast Portland with his wife, Mirela, and his daughter, Norah and co-author of *Raised? Finding Jesus by Doubting the Resurrection.*

Winfield Bevins is Founding Pastor of Church of the Outer Banks and the author of several books. He speaks at conferences, workshops, and retreats throughout the United States on a variety of topics. He has a Doctorate from Southeastern Seminary in Wake Forest, NC.

Matt Oakes is a musician from Austin, TX. He is married to Joanie and dad to Bella, Imogen, and Noah. Matt received his B.S. in Worship Arts from Corban College and is completing his M.Div. at Redeemer Seminary, Austin.

Stephen Witmer (PhD, University of Cambridge) is Pastor of Pepperell Christian Fellowship in Pepperell, MA and teaches

New Testament at Gordon-Conwell Theological Seminary. He is the author of *Eternity Changes Everything: How to live now in the light of your future* (Good Book Company), and has written for *Themelios*, Reformation 21, Bible Study Magazine, Desiring God, and The Gospel Coalition.

Greg Willson is married to Christina and lives in Columbia, SC. He is interested in church planting, the arts, and writing.

Mathew B. Sims is the author of *A Household Gospel: Fulfilling the Great Commission in Our Homes* and writes for The Council on Biblical Manhood & Womanhood, Gospel-Centered Discipleship, Borrowed Light, and other publications. He also works as the Managing Editor at Gospel-Centered Discipleship and offers freelance editing and book formatting services.

Matt Manry is the Director of Discipleship at Life Bible Church in Canton, GA. He is a student at Reformed Theological Seminary and Knox Theological Seminary. He is also an editor for Credo Magazine and Gospel-Centered Discipleship.

Nick Rynerson is a staff writer for Christ and Pop Culture and a marketing coordinator at Crossway Books in Wheaton, IL. He graduated from Illinois State University and is married to his lovely wife, Jenna.

Abe Meysenburg serves as a pastor-elder with Soma Tacoma in Tacoma, WA, as well as serving on board for the larger Soma Family of Churches. He is a graduate of Moody Bible Institute, and is married to Jennifer. They have four children: Abby, Julia, Luke, and Noah.

Lindsay Powell Fooshee is married to John, and together they serve Jesus in East Tennessee through church planting. They are passionate about discipling their four kids, who challenge them to soak up the daily joys of toddlers and teenagers at the same time. Lindsay holds an M.A. in Christian Thought from Gordon-Conwell Theological Seminary.

J. A. Medders is the Lead Pastor of Redeemer Church in Tomball, TX. He and Natalie have two kids, Ivy and Oliver. Jeff's first book, *Gospel Formed: Living a Grace-Addicted, Truth-Filled, Jesus-Exalting Life*, is set to release on Nov, 27, 2014 from Kregel.

Brent Thomas lives with his wife Kristi and their eight children in Glendale, AZ. He serves as an elder with Church of the Cross and as Area Vice President, Church Relations for Apartment Life.

Danielle Brooks lives in St. Augustine, Florida where she owns and operates Danielle Brooks Photography. In their free time, Danielle and her husband, Rich, love to travel. They attend Coquina Community Church and host various weekly gatherings in their home. They are also parents to a crazy Russian Blue cat named Ava.

Joey Cochran is the husband of Kendall and father of three. He graduated from Dallas Seminary and is the church planting intern at Redeemer Fellowship St. Charles under Joe Thorn's supervision.

OTHER RESOURCES
from GCD Books

Visit GCDiscipleship.com

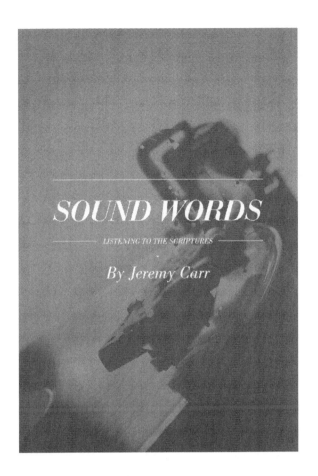

Sounds Words by Jeremy Carr

"The church continues to need an understanding of discipleship that draws people to love and know God. This book delivers. It is an accessible and practical theology of scripture for discipleship. Jeremy is not exhorting you to love the Bible more, but declaring that God's love for you causes you to know and love him and his Word more."

JUSTIN S. HOLCOMB
Adjunct Professor of Theology and
Philosophy, Reformed Theological Seminary

Gospel Amensia by Luma Simms

"Luma Simms remembers vividly what it was like to be simply going through the motions of a spiritual life. She writes like someone who has just been awakened from a nightmare and can still describe it in detail. Luma's voice communicates the pain of forgetting what matters most, and may be just the voice to reach the half-awake."

FRED SANDERS
Associate Professor of Theology,
Torrey Honors Institute, Biola University

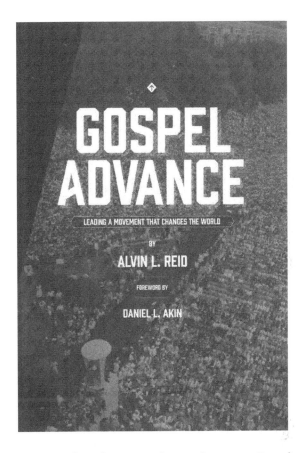

Gospel Advance by Alvin L. Reid

"*Gospel Advance* is Alvin Reid's challenge to the Church to recover our mission focus and advance a movement of God
through the gospel. Reading this book is like sitting down across
from this passionate evangelism professor and hearing from his
heart. He describes the history of evangelical awakenings and
prescribes a way forward for 21st century believers. May the
Lord use this work to ignite your heart for the nations!"

TREVIN WAX
Managing Editor of *The Gospel Project*
author of *Counterfeit Gospels*

everPresent by Jeremy Writebol

"*everPresent* does something that most books don't achieve in today's theological landscape. Most focus either on who God is or what we should do. Jeremy's efforts start with who God is to walk the reader down the path of what God has done, who we are because of God, and then, logically and succinctly, points us to naturally understand what we are to do because of this. I highly recommend picking this book up to better understand both the why and how of the life of those that follow Jesus."

SETH MCBEE
Executive Team Member, GCM Collective

Made in the USA
Charleston, SC
24 July 2014